INTERACTION IN EVERYDAY LIFE
Social Strategies

Edited by
JOHN LOFLAND

SAGE PUBLICATIONS   *Beverly Hills / London*   **1978**

The material in this publication originally appeared in URBAN LIFE AND CULTURE, July 1972 (Volume 1, Number 2), October 1972 (Volume 1, Number 3), January 1974 (Volume 2, Number 4), and, retitled URBAN LIFE, July 1976 (Volume 5, Number 2); also in SOCIOLOGY OF WORK AND OCCUPATIONS, August 1976 (Volume 3, Number 3). The Publisher would like to acknowledge the assistance of the editors of these journals, John Lofland, John Irwin, and Rue Bucher, in making this edition possible.

For information address:

SAGE PUBLICATIONS, INC.
275 South Beverly Drive
Beverly Hills, California 90212

SAGE PUBLICATIONS LTD
28 Banner Street
London EC1Y 8QE, England

Printed in the United States of America

International Standard Book Number 0-8039-1035-5

Library of Congress Catalog Number 78-51495

FIRST PRINTING

CONTENTS

INTRODUCTION: *The Qualitative Strategy*

Approach to Interaction in Everyday Life

JOHN LOFLAND

A BASIC (AND HAPPILY PRACTICAL) sociological question is: What are the techniques by means of which people manage the situations of their everyday lives? Starting from the assumption that no social arrangement simply "is," but must constantly be constructed, what are the unceasingly produced and placed building blocks from which the structures of social life are unremittingly fabricated?

There are, of course, diverse (and conflicting) approaches to answering this question. In this volume, I single out and focus on one major approach in the hope of clarifying its nature and potential by means of conveniently collected, concrete research illustrations. Conceived most broadly, the approach may be thought of as a symbolic interactionist answer to the question of doing social life (Blumer, 1969). However, symbolic interactionists ask more than this question and not all interactionists would answer it in the way I will shortly describe. More narrowly, therefore, the approach offered here may be thought of as a "qualitative strategy" perspective on the hows of constructing social life. The term "qualitative" points to the approach's conception of a useful form of knowledge and correspondingly appropriate method. The form of knowledge (discussed below as principle #1) may be captioned "disciplined abstractions." Appropriate methods involve a special kind of "intimate familiarity" (principle #2, below). The term "strategy" points to a particular conception of human action and provides a guide to collecting and analyzing data gained by intimate familiarity and developed into disciplined abstractions. This conception and guide involves the idea of a "situation" on the one side (principle #3, below) and of strategy, on the other side (principle #4, below).

Jointly executed, these four elements form a qualitative strategy perspective for studying how people do social things.

CONSTITUTIONAL PRINCIPLES OF SOCIOLOGY

The qualitative strategy approach is itself, however, but one variation on more basic sociological analysis, and it assumes several more general or constitutional principles of sociology. In order to avoid confusion, it is best to at least mention the more salient principles of sociology that are logically prior to the specific qualitative strategy approach and not at all unique to it.

First, sociology is the study of social organization, the trans-personal ways in which people are interrelated. Units of social organization range from the immediate, micro, face-to-face encounter, through relationships, small groups, organizations and settlements, up through entire societies. In this volume, we deal almost entirely with the encounter-scale of human social organization—immediate, face-to-face contact, including inter-action with oneself (as seen in Bernstein, in this volume).

Second, sociological analysis searches for the generic rather than the merely topical, for underlying, widely occurring forms of social organization, of situations and strategies. Thus, in the papers of this volume, typical settings are such things as schools, public places, doors, traffic courts, and the like. But each of the papers also has a generic focus, as in the concepts of student fritters, accounts, cultivated relationships, the guided options management strategy, and bad news.

Third, products of inquiry must always be judged against the background of what is already "common sense" or otherwise known about some generic aspect of social organization. That is, sociological inquiry is best justified when it goes beyond the obvious and explicitly aims to find (and does find) something new or novel (M. Davis, 1971). This often involves looking at the commonplace, but looking at it in new ways, as is done in most of the papers reprinted here.

The principles of focusing upon the social organizational, the generic, and the novel provide an orienting framework that constrains and channels the four principles of the qualitative strategy approach.

PRINCIPLES OF THE QUALITATIVE
STRATEGY APPROACH

The *first* principle of the qualitative strategy approach is that social data are appropriately collected by means of intimate familiarity by which is meant close, detailed, dense acquaintanceship with a particular locale of social life based on free-flowing and prolonged immersion. This immersion, first and ideally, may take the form of direct, bodily presence in the physical scenes of the social life under scrutiny, either in an indigenous role or in the role of someone known to be studying that world. This relation is known technically to social scientists as "participant-observation" (Lofland, 1971: ch. 5). All seven of the inquiries in this volume employed some form of participant observation.

Though not ideal, a practical degree of intimate familiarity can often be attained by a second means—namely, long, diverse, open-ended, semi-structured conversations with people who are participants in a situation or social world. Since some kinds of situations are not readily amenable to direct physical participation by analysts of them, selected participants must be induced to sit down for many hours, to discuss a wide range of concrete matters they confront and to talk about how they act toward them. Unlike more conventional "interviewing," which is oriented importantly to attitudes, "intensive interviewing" is oriented to collecting instances and episodes of action and instances and episodes of problems and how they are dealt with. A goal of intensive or "qualitative" interviewing is to construct records of action-in-process from a variety of people who have likely performed these actions time and time again. Key features of such "conversations" are their length and diversity. Unhurried, free-flowing talk encourages the emergence of a wide range and many levels of topics, prompting intimate familiarity (Lofland, 1971: ch. 4; Bogdan and Taylor, 1975). Third and slightly marginal, a mass of qualitative, written documents can sometimes provide usable intimate familiarity.

Such intimate familiarity is needed in order for the investigator to confront the life under study on its own terms and thereby to avoid the mere elaboration of preexisting stereotypes about it (Lofland, 1976: ch.2).

Intimate familiarity arising from participant observation or qualitative interviewing is, during the process of its achievement (and after), subjected to effort to develop "disciplined abstractions," the *second* principle. The principle of disciplined abstractions requires, first, the accumulation of a rich, written record of situation- and strategy-relevent episodes, incidents, events, exchanges, remarks, happenings, conversations, and the like. Data are collected by means of attending to and recording the running episodes of everyday life. Procedurally, the analyst is a compulsive looker, reader, and notetaker (and/or intensive interviewer and tape recording transcriber), building up perhaps hundreds or thousands of pages of episodes. Either during the observation/interviewing/reading period or after, the episodes are sorted and classified, re-sorted, and reclassified until a faithful and detailed analysis is achieved. (Since the minute procedural and technical details of these processes of "partici-

pant observation," "intensive interviewing," and other techniques of qualitative analysis are reasonably straightforward and
are amply described in standard manuals, I will not dwell on
technical aspects. See Lofland, 1971: ch. 6; Bogdan and Taylor,
1975; Schatzman and Strauss, 1973.)

Because of the intimate interplay between perspective (situa-
tion-strategy notions in the present context), the accumulating
qualitative data, and the emergent abstractions, written reports
have an interpenetrated character; that is, the abstractions and
qualitative data coexist as one whole. Each depends on the
other for enlightenment and meaning. Taken separately, the
abstractions and data may have slight interest or merit. The
abstractions are likely to be dull because the reader has an inadequate conception of the concrete, empirical reality to which
they might refer. The qualitative data alone are dull because the
reader has little notion of generic patterns involved, save those
he might himself be imposing. But interpenetration through
minute and continual alternation between abstraction and episodes makes the whole more than the parts.

Each of the studies below well illustrates this interpenetration, and each is usefully examined from this standpoint alone.
Each continually alternates between (a) abstract categories of
situational features and types of generic strategies and (b)
description of concrete things that people are doing that em-
body these abstract categories. Abstractions are continually
"touched down" by concrete instances, because in developing
analysis, concrete instances have "touched off" abstractions. In
this sense, the concrete and the abstract coexist.

These first two principles are founded on the epistemological
conviction that effective human thought and action are best facilitated by disciplined alternation between the abstract and the
concrete. To deal only at the level of the concrete is to be a
prisoner of minutiae—not to see the forest for the trees. To deal
only at the level of the abstract is to be limited to empirically
empty concepts—to deal in floating, airy, mental entities di-
vorced from empirical reality. Each direction alone is sterile. It
is through the intimate interplay of the concrete and the abstract that knowledge, understanding, and action are most
effectively developed.

Intimate familiarity and disciplined abstractions about what? In this case, about situation and strategies.

The *third* principle is that of focusing on the situation. The analyst asks about the concrete location in the world with which he or she is becoming intimately familiar: With what (generic and hopefully novel) set of things do people here have to deal? Scrutiny of the seven studies in this volume will show that each has an initial section outlining a more or less generic situation. My caption-summary of each situation is indicated in the first half of each title that I have provided in the table of contents. For example, I caption Stan Bernstein's paper as dealing with "the situation of the never-ending task," and so on for the other chapters.

Reports of qualitatively studied strategies often and appropriately open with a description of the generic situation studied, as Odis Bigus does admirably in his paper in this volume on cultivation and the milkman.

Articulate studies employing a qualitative strategy perspective are being completed at an accelerating rate. My own recent, incomplete, and almost instantly outdated survey of such studies chronicles more than hundred (Lofland, 1976: chs. 8-11). It is therefore becoming more and more relevant to ask how such studies can and should themselves best be accumulated and consolidated. One possible direction is in terms of the most basic and generic situations to which they are addressed. There do not yet appear to be enough studies on any given generic situation to make a quantum leap in analysis, but such a time may not be far off for at least one or two generic situations. In reviewing qualitative strategy materials for this Sage Contemporary Social Science Anthology, I was impressed with the recurrence of three possibly generic situations in the materials of several Sage journals, especially *Urban Life,* from which the papers reprinted here are mostly drawn. It is in terms of these three recurrences that I have thought it best to present selected inquiries.

The first of these is solitude in the form of literally "no-other-body" present or of other-bodies-present but not engaged in spoken interaction. Bernstein's statement on fritters is a brilliant explication of socially naked self-management in the former sense. Analysis of self-management (over "the American dilemma") is also nicely carried forward by Caditz (1977). Lyn Lofland has pioneered the empirical explication of solitude in public places (in this volume, and 1972), work that has been usefully augmented by Henderson (1975) and Karp (1973). Elements in the process of going from solitude to encounter in the context of sexual pairing in public places are reported by Cloyd (1976).

The situation of subordination is a second and more heavily worked area. I suppose it is not surprising to find that the situations and strategies of subordinate *occupations* have attracted particular attention, reflecting as they do the social locations from which sociologists are drawn and their relative ease of access. Thus, we have the suggestive studies of Bigus on the milkman, Slosar on bus drivers (1973), Mayer and Rosenblatt on social workers (1975), Christopherson on art photographers (1974a, 1974b,), and Holtz on the professional bridge player (1975). In the legal context, the situation and strategies of traffic court grievers (Coleman, this volume) and drunken drivers (Warren and Phillips, 1976) have been conceived in promising ways. Sexual subordination is of course generically identical to these other topical forms and is well exemplified in Walum's depiction of the situation of face-to-face "authority etiquette" (this volume) and in Davis and Davis's ferreting out of how women cope with erotically offensive men (1976). While not tightly qualitative field work in character, Warner, Wellman and Weitzman's (1973) consolidation of many statements in terms of the basic postures subordinates may strike stands as an indispensable guidepost in the continuing study of subordinates.

Subordinates imply superordinates, and their generic situation is the third major focus. The articulately qualitative strategy materials I have noticed in recent Sage Publications journals have dealt with occupational contexts of superordination. Reflecting, perhaps, the large-scale and specialized aspects of American society, these studies also deal heavily with superordinates who are relative *strangers* to the people they superordinate, and the studies deal, moreover, with situations of crises. Thus, Coombs and Powers (1975) report strategies of physicians in learning to cope with patient death; Charmaz (1975) delineates coroners' methods of announcing death; Roth (1972) focuses on staff (and client) techniques of control in hospital emergency rooms; McClenahen and Lofland (this volume) look at how deputy U.S. Marshals bear bad news; and, Larsen (1975) depicts how foundations decipher the mysteries of applicant proposals to spend foundation money. On the side of more ordinary life, Dixon (this volume) insightfully analyzes the "guided options" management strategy by means of which adult caretakers control children in a pre-school and Izraeli (1977) lays bare methods by means of which new managers do or do not get control of new subordinates.

Of course, these are not the only or perhaps even the most important generic situations of social life. Others include the situation of equality and the various major transitions of the life cycle such as the first pregnancy, the geographic move, and the retirement (Hamburg, Coelho, and Adams, 1974: 424).

Irrespective of the specific generic situation, the larger and longer-term goal is to accumulate qualitative situation and strategy studies sufficient then to undertake systematic comparison and contrast (Lofland, 1976: ch. 7).

The *fourth* principle of the qualitative strategy approach is but the logical next step: a focus on strategies. Action does not simply happen, it has to be *constructed.* Every situation has an ongoing structure of contrivances, gambits, maneuvers, mechanisms, ploys, tacks, tactics, or whatever terms one prefers.

Interaction strategies display differences of *scale,* differences in the amount of time, space, and equipment employed and the number of people involved. The simplest, shortest ones that involve only one or a few people acting over but a few seconds, minutes, or hours may be termed *encounter-scale* strategies. As indicated earlier, virtually all the interaction strategies reported in this volume are at the encounter-scale. Multiple-people cooperating over days, weeks, months, or longer are implementing group, organization, or even larger scales of interaction strategy (Lofland, 1976: chs. 8-11).

The term strategy implies conscious intention, as well it should since people very often do consciously deliberate and strategize their action. In studying interaction strategies, though, we must be careful not to confine our conception of strategy only to action the participants consciously conceive as such. Much action has strategic *significance* and import in situations even if it lacks strategic intention, as is illustrated in all the following reports, especially those by Lyn Lofland on public places and Odis Bigus on milkmen. One way we know action is strategic without being so intended is the easy willingness with which people often acknowledge such significance (import, function, or consequence) when we call it to their attention. Consider in this light, specifically, Lyn Lofland's portrayal of public place self-management (this volume and 1972) and your likely new and conscious conception of the strategic significance of your own behavior in public places.

Relative to the form of organizing a report, the section on strategies commonly follows the section on the situation and makes up the bulk of the paper. This is the case with all of the reprinted studies that follow. Moreover, the better to communicate both the strategies at hand and to facilitate eventual consolidation with other studies on the same generic situation, it is helpful to name or otherwise clearly to signal the reported strategies. The seven studies presented in this volume were selected in part because of their articulate clarity in this respect.

It is, then, out of the interplay between abstract sensitivities and hundreds of episodes that an emergent generic delineation of a situation and its strategies has the character of being grounded in the concrete reality of the empirical world. The analyst

   (1) begins with an abstract sense of what a generic situation is and what generic strategies are;
   (2) immerses himself in the concrete items of the actual social life under study;
   (3) develops and constructs a generically framed analysis of situations and strategies from the organic intertwining of items 1 and 2.

Qualitative strategy analysts are simultaneously deductive (situations and strategies are "directives") and inductive (episodes are the unanalyzed data), a straddling that Glaser and Strauss (1967) have aptly termed a "grounded" approach.

Each of the papers presented here well exemplifies this process and represents a patiently empirical approach to answering the question stated in the opening sentence of this introduction: "What are the techniques by means of which people manage the situations of their everyday lives?"

REFERENCES

BLUMER, H. (1969) Symbolic Interactionism. Englewood Cliffs, NJ: Prentice-Hall.

BOGDAN, R. and S. J. TAYLOR (1975) Introduction to Qualitative Research Methods. New York: John Wiley.

CADITZ, J. (1977) "Coping with the American dilemma: dissonance reduction among white liberals." Pacific Soc. Rev. 20: 21-42.

CHARMAZ, K. C. (1975) "The coroner's strategies for announcing death." Urban Life 4: 296-316.

CHRISTOPHERSON, R. W. (1974a) "Making art with machines: photography's institutional inadequacies." Urban Life 3: 3-34.

––– (1974b) "From folk art to fine art: a transformation in the meaning of photographic work." Urban Life 3: 123-157.

CLOYD, J. W. (1976) "The market-place bar: the interrelation between sex, situation, and strategies in the pairing ritual of homo ludens." Urban Life 5: 293-312.

COOMBS, R. H. and P. S. POWERS (1975) "Socialization for death; the physican's role." Urban Life 4: 250-271.

DAVIS, M. (1971) "That's interesting." Philosophy of Sci. 1: 309-344.

DAVIS, S. K. and P. W. DAVIS (1976) "Meanings and process in erotic offensiveness: an exposé of exposés." Urban Life 5: 377-396.

GLASER, B. and A. STRAUSS (1967) The Discovery of Grounded Theory. Chicago: Aldine.

HAMBURG, D., G. COELHO, and J. ADAMS (1974) "Coping and adaptation," pp. 419-424, in G. Coelho, D. Hamburg, and J. Adams (eds.) Coping and Adaptation. New York: Basic Books.

HENDERSON, M. R. (1975) "Acquiring privacy in public." Urban Life 3: 446-455.

HOLTZ, J. A. (1975) "The professional duplicate bridge player: conflict management in a free, legal quasi-deviant occupation." Urban Life 4: 131-148.

IZRAELI, D. (1977) "Settling-in: an interactionist perspective on the entry of the new manager." Pacific Soc. Rev. 20: 135-160.

KARP, D. A. (1973) "Hiding in pornographic bookstores: reconsideration of the nature of urban anonymity." Urban Life 1: 427-451.

LARSEN, K. (1975) "Foundation managers, candidates, and grantees: a study of classification and control." Urban Life 3: 396-441.

LOFLAND, J. (1976) Doing Social Life: The Qualitative Study of Human Interaction in Natural Settings. New York: Wiley-Interscience.
––– (1971) Analyzing Social Settings. Belmont, CA: Wadsworth.
LOFLAND, L. H. (1972) "Self-management in public settings: part I." Urban Life 1: 93-108.
MAYER, J. E. and A. ROSENBLATT (1975) "Encounters with danger: social workers in the ghetto." Sociology of Work and Occupations 2: 227-256.
McCLENAHEN, L. and J. LOFLAND (1976) "Bearing bad news; tactics of the deputy U.S. Marshal." Sociology of Work and Occupations, 3: 251-272.
SCHATZMAN, L. and A. STRAUSS (1973) Field Research. Englewood Cliffs, NJ: Prentice-Hall.
SLOSAR, J. A. (1973) "Ogre, bandit, and operating employee: the problems and adaptations of the metropolitan bus driver." Urban Life 1: 339-362.
ROTH, J. A. (1972) "Staff and client control strategies in urban hospital emergency services." Urban Life 1: 39-60.
WARNER, R. S., D. T. WELLMAN, and L. J. WEITZMAN (1973) "The hero, the sambo, and the operator: three characterizations of the oppressed." Urban Life 2: 53-84.
WARREN, C. A. B. and S. W. PHILLIPS (1976) "Stigma negotiation: expression games, accounts, and the drunken driver." Urban Life 5: 53-74.

I. SOLITUDE

It is useful to distinguish two forms of solitude: physical aloneness in the literal sense and being interactionally alone although in the physical presence of others. Physical solitude accentuates the need of the individual to manage his relation to himself and reveals "self-management" in perhaps the purest sense of that term. Stan Bernstein marvelously documents several aspects of such self-machination. In contrast, social solitude (specifically, being alone in the presence of strangers) brings forth an astonishing range of efforts to take account of other people even though these others are in several social senses "not there." Lyn Lofland refers to this subterranean attending as "self-management," but we need to be equally impressed with it as "other-management," albeit other-management at a distance.

STAN BERNSTEIN is an advanced graduate student in the Doctoral Program in Social Psychology, The University of Michigan. His major theoretical interests are in the areas of commitment, resocialization, and non-verbal communication. He is currently doing field research on commitment and intensive resocialization.

GETTING IT DONE: *Notes on Student Fritters*

STAN BERNSTEIN

SOCIAL ROLES VARY in the degree to which their constituent tasks are "closed" or "open" in character. At one extreme are roles such as assembly-line worker, where precise definitions communicate when the task starts, one's progress in it, and when it ends. At the other extreme are roles such as student, where the tasks are highly open or never-ending. The role of student, in particular, involves learning to think and learning the "facts" of various fields. The infinite expandibility of these tasks places no practically determined restrictions on the amount of time occupants can dedicate to the role. Like politicians, housewives, and other entrepreneurs, students' work is never done. Indeed, students are counselled that people only stop learning when they die. Death is not, students lament, in sight, but learning demands are.

This paper seeks to explore how people cope with roles that are open or never-ending in their demands. In particular, it

AUTHOR'S NOTE: The author acknowledges the invaluable assistance of Mr. Jeff Hart (Boston College) in the development of the idea of fritter. Special thanks are due Ms. Susan Wilcox for assistance.

[17]

focuses upon how students justify not working under the ever-present pressure to work. Frequently, when there is work to be done, students fritter away time. An analysis of strategies students adopt in accounting for their time not working will be presented. The objective truth or falsity of the strategies is irrelevant to the purpose of this analysis. What is important is their use in coping with open-ended situations.

NEUTRALIZATION, ACCOUNTS, AND FRITTERS

The present effort both follows and departs from prior research. Matza (1964) discusses how an individual in a subculture of delinquents neutralizes his guilt over performing delinquent acts. Relevant here, Matza notes that the delinquent's relation to the norms he violates includes strong elements of normative acceptance. It is not sheer rejection of legal norms but, for most, ambivalence or acceptance with definitions of extenuating. circumstances. Students' attitudes toward normatively expected study are also frequently complex and ambivalent. Matza notes that delinquents only occasionally commit delinquent acts. Intermittent violation is also a characteristic of most students' work avoidance.

An important element in Matza's discussion is the fact that neutralization techniques are common in the subculture of delinquency as a way of freeing the individual from moral constraint in violating legal norms. The legal system is the one which labels the acts deviant. The relationship of the definitions of justified action of the delinquent groups to the social control agents' definitions is studied. In individual role management, however, the individual is his own social control agent. It is not clear whether the neutralizations in Matza's discussion are to be considered as justified accounts to others (especially members of one's own group), or primarily as accounts to self.

A more general presentation of accounts can be found in the excellent treatments by Scott and Lyman (1970, 1968). In introducing their discussion, they present the study of accounts as necessary for an understanding of the maintaining of social order after failure to meet social expectations. How does the individual explain his act to others when he has not met their expectations?

(1) How does he excuse his wrong action (escape responsibility) or,

(2) how does he justify his behavior (neutralize the pejorative portrayal of the consequences)?

Accounts repair the breaks in satisfying the expectations of others. Scott and Lyman's presentation is complex. Group differences in acceptable accounts, the style of accounts, audience selection for accounts, and many other questions are sensitively handled. The relation of accounts given to others and accounts offered to self in role management is, however, not discussed. Accounts are considered part of a sociology of talk. An account is "a statement made by a social actor to explain unanticipated or untoward behavior—whether the behavior is his own or that of others, and whether the proximate cause for the statement arises from the actor himself or someone else" (Scott and Lyman, 1968: 46). To their discussion, I here add that the recipient of the account may be the actor himself. Further, an explanation may succeed as an account only for the actor.

This analysis treats a student population. It is this population that the author knows best from years of active participation as an undergraduate and graduate student, and, as a teacher of undergraduates in two college settings. The central notion is that of fritter devices or strategies. A fritter is "a justification a student gives to himself for not doing student work in response to felt pressures to work." While the success of a fritter in neutralizing work pressure or guilt is increased by its receiving social support, this consideration is not part of the definition.

The dynamic nature of fritters makes categorizing them difficult. In actual practice, combinations or complex sequences are likely as the student continually reconstitutes his work-avoiding as new kinds of justified activity. For ease of presentation, they may be divided into four classes: (1) person-based; (2) social relations-based; (3) valuative-based; and (4) task-based.

PERSON-BASED FRITTERS

Person-based fritters involve definitions of biological need and personal history.

Biological Necessity

Even a student is human. Being human involves, among other things, the satisfaction of biological needs. These practical necessities are just that—necessities. Therefore, they are fool-proof justifications for not working. When, for example, nature calls, what is a person to do but respond to his mother's entreaty? Similarly, hunger can serve as a justification for work avoidance. Not only can an argument be made for biological necessity, but the student can also argue that hunger impairs studying ability. This argument need not be limited, of course, by actual hunger. The great business done by vending machines in dormitories and the concentration of all-night eating places in areas of high student residence attest to the utility of this justification. Some popular student foods (pizza in particular) are not eaten alone. Time must be spent gathering other people. And once you have them, you can do more with them than eat.

Cleanliness is yet another excellent justification. Anything next to godliness surely takes precedence over work. Washing and showering can serve another function. An entire battery of work-avoidance tactics can be justified by their necessity in keeping the student awake. These activities include preparing and drinking cups of coffee, cold showers, long walks in cold weather, running a half-mile, standing on one's head for a few minutes, listening to Sousa marches, Chopin preludes, or acid rock, and eating rich food. A variety of drugs are now routinely used to fight fatigue. The effects of these are frequently not restricted to fatigue reduction. Subtle and not very subtle alterations of consciousness are common. Attending to these changes can become more interesting than studying. Should these activities fail, or even should they succeed, another way of handling "fatigue" is the I'll-get-up-very-early-tomorrow-morning-when-I'll-be-able-to-work-better fritter. Students have to keep healthy, too. Many regimens, physical and medical, may be required. At some times, it may be crucial that the student get "adequate rest."

Rest on Your Laurels

Focusing on personal history leads to the nostalgia or rest-on-your-laurels fritter. Using this strategy involves employing past accomplishments as justification for present work avoidance. This can take the form of delaying work, since previous history shows (or can be interpreted to suggest) it well within one's capability and therefore not a matter of pressing concern. Or when the present activity proves frustrating to the point of work avoidance, the individual may bolster his esteem by "celebrating" previous successes. A variant on this theme is especially handy for avoiding work when a number of different tasks must be done. Upon completion of one of them, the student may use a you-owe-it-to-yourself justification for work avoidance, the avoidance period being defined as self-payment for a job well done.

An owe-it-to-yourself break may also be seen as necessary to let the worker change psychological set or recover from fatigue. More work is more fatiguing than almost any nonwork activity. It is easier to change set to most nonwork acts than to most other work.

SOCIAL RELATIONS-BASED FRITTERS

Fritters based upon social relations directly employ other people in the action of avoiding work. The impact of employing other people, however, is not so much in having an audience before which one gives accounts as simply in having an audience. There are three main patterns of social relations fritters.

Group Discussion

The group-discussion fritter is also called the commiseration fritter. Commiserating may be done in a large group or in pairs either in person or over the telephone. It involves "getting together" and consoling one another on the unreasonability or irrationality of the assignment. Complaining about the assigned work is an excellent fritter technique. It justifies work avoidance by directly protesting against the work itself. The more intelligent or discriminating the complaints, the clearer it is that the work task is within the student's later capability. Critical ability may be developed in avoiding studying as well as in doing studying. Sometimes discussions of this sort get around to a comparison of actual work done, leading to the social-comparison fritter.

Social Comparison

Students sometimes compare their progress with one another. When a student discovers he is ahead of others in his work, he can then feel justified in freeing time for work avoidance. This fritter has two aspects. First, there is the time spent gathering comparisons of others. This may involve personal contact or telephoning. Or the comparison others may not be real others working on the same task. Instead, high relative standing earlier in the course may be extrapolated to the present. Because of information from the past, the student may believe he is at present ahead of others. When this is coupled with the perception that relative position is the criterion of final evaluation, it becomes possible, for example, for "curve-breaking" midterm students to free time from final studies and projects. Second, there is the effect of the comparison. The choice of comparison others is a strategic choice. For a student to feel justified in his current work avoidance, he must compare his work with someone who is less advanced than he. (Choice of other will vary depending on whether the student wishes to take a break from work or gain incentive to continue it.) The two dangers of this technique for the student are: first, he may choose someone who is, in fact, more advanced in the work; and, second, he may fritter away the time needed for students to catch up and pass him. This second possibility exists because, in seeking a justification for work avoidance, students frequently stop at discovering they are ahead, do not collect information on the rate of progress of others, and thus easily misestimate the time it takes others to close the gap. This problem is less threatening and the fritter more successful if the time before the deadline is small. One possible result of such a technique is to make distributions of student performance more closely approximate the normal curve than would otherwise be the case.

Group Work

The decision to study in a group has a number of work-avoidance functions. On the one hand, it immediately makes possible commiseration and social-comparison fritters. Study groups from the same course can, of course, commiserate easily. Students studying together, but for different courses, are able to have even longer commiseration sessions. Each can complain about his course without redundancy and without risk of contradiction or challenge. Social-comparison fritters are also possible both as a group enterprise in relation to a group-defined standard of adequate knowledge for the course and as a sort of distributive justice notion for comparison between courses with groups of students studying for different courses. A group norm of "reasonable work for any course" can then develop independent of the actual demands of the actual courses being studied.

Getting a number of people together functions, on the other hand, to increase enormously the range of alternatives to studying. These activities can be justified using any number of the techniques elsewhere mentioned. Work avoidance maneuvers with group approval are especially difficult to ignore. There is a "risky shift" in the direction of longer fritters, too. This is because, once you have stopped working, it is difficult to know when to suggest to your partners that you should get back to work. It may be hard to stop frittering without being impolite or pressuring. Responsibility for directing attention back to work becomes diffused through the group.

VALUATIVE-BASED FRITTERS

While the above-mentioned fritter techniques are common and successful, they do not have the guilt-binding power of valuative fritters. One way work can be avoided especially, but not exclusively, in the early college years is using time to discuss values. Political, moral, and aesthetic topics are common in these conversations. Finding out who you are, "getting your shit together," and so on is an important task. Mundane work considerations do not look very important measured against this larger activity. Valuative fritters based on already-held values place work and work avoidance within a larger framework of values and choices. It is here that considerations of nonstudent activities enter with greatest effect. Three primary types of valuative fritters may be described and ordered in terms of increasing generality and abstraction.

Higher Good

In the higher-good work-avoidance strategy, the student ranks being a student as less important to him in his scheme of values than other interests and aspects of his identity. Here friendship, love, cultural values (e.g., charity, service), political interests, physical fitness (the sound-mind-in-a-sound-body frit-ter), and much else can be justified as more worthy of attention for the moment than the study tasks at hand. These other values, of course, vary in strength and, therefore, in their guilt-free binding power in role management. For this reason, the strength of each of the alternative values is enhanced immeasurably if it can be asserted that the opportunity for acting on that value is soon to be gone. Stated another way, *rare events,* or at least infrequent events, have a special ability to bind time from studying, even if the value of the act would otherwise be questionable in relation to the pressure to study. Makes-Jack-a-dull-boy valuative fritters, involving, say, a movie, will be more potent the last day the picture is playing than the first day of an extended run, concerts involving great and infrequently heard performers are able to appease guilt from role violation, and eclipses of the moon draw crowds of guilt-free students as an audience.

Experience Broadens

The experience-broadens fritter is less specific in the sense of presenting a less clear-cut value conflict. It has, nonetheless, the attraction of serving as a ready back-up to a post-facto unjustified valuative fritter (say, the movie was lousy, the instruments out of tune, the friend crabby, the eclipse cloud-ridden, or what have you). In such an event, or generally in any event, it can be argued somehow that experience qua experience broadens the person, makes him more complete, or wiser, or what have you. This can bind successfully enormous amounts of time on a scale much larger than the mere work requirements for a specific course. Even career decisions (or decision evasions) can be justified under the experience-broadens rubric. The crucial difference from the higher-good fritter is that any experience will do.

Existential

The most general of valuative fritters is the existential, or the what-the-hell-sort-of-difference-will-it-make fritter. In this strategy, the decision to work or not work is cast as having no lasting practical or existential effect on the course of one's life (or, sometimes, other's, as in the would-be author's no-one-will-be-reading-novels-in-ten-years-anyway fritter). Scholastic failures of prominently successful individuals may be remembered. Einstein's failure of a high school math course can offer solace to the fritterer. If one's activities are ultimately of no consequence anyway, the immediate consequences of work avoidance are not even worthy of consideration. Extreme application of this principle can lead to failure in the student role, in which event one's very studenthood may be justified as an experience-broadens fritter from what one should really be doing.

TASK-BASED FRITTERS

Fritters discussed to this point are based upon the student's history, biology, social relations, and values. We come finally to the task itself. Task-based fritters focus upon the direct handling of study time and the allocation of work resources. Specifically, there appear to be four main clusters of task-based fritters: time-related; preparation-related; creativity-related; and task-involved.

Time-Related Fritters

THE TIME SYMMETRY FRITTER

Many students appear to find it easier to start studying on the hour, half-hour, or, at the very least, quarter-hour than at any other minute. This may be due to the ease these times make for scheduling fritters discussed below. These times are more generally important in plans and schedules between individuals. A common social use of time shapes action. (On a larger scale, weekends, holidays, or Mondays assume special status in the week.) It is, further, "easier" to compute total study time and pages per hour if you start at some such prominent time division. One of the advantages of this technique is that, with a little effort, a large amount of time can be frittered if the activity one chose to do until, say, the quarter-hour starting time, can be extended just a few minutes beyond this starting point. The student is then, by the same logic, justified in waiting until the next prominent time division. Depending on the individual and on the amount of time already spent in time symmetry fritters, the student can choose to wait for the next hour, half-hour, or quarter-hour. As good a fritter technique as this is, there is a problem in its use. Each time it is used in succession, the student feels less justified in invoking the time symmetry fritter. This is sometimes manifested by the setting of the starting time at progressively shorter prominent intervals: e.g., at 7:00, 8:00, 8:30, and then 8:45. In any event, at some point, this technique loses its efficacy. Fortunately, there is a larger-scale, more successful technique which can then be used.

THE GREAT DIVIDE FRITTER

At some point, say, in an evening to be devoted to work, it becomes too late to get serious work done (or finish the task, the scheduled amount, or what have you). At this point, the student feels perfectly free to give up for the rest of the night all pretense to studying. It is simply too late to get enough work done to make any work worthwhile. Some other activity is then chosen to occupy the remaining time, but without any need for a higher-good valuative justification. Thus, a particular student might not consider it worthwhile to start studying after 9:00 at night. The time-symmetry fritter brought the student up to 8:45, a biological-imperative fritter or a phone-call-for-a-commiseration fritter might be sufficient to add enough time to set up a great divide fritter.

SCHEDULING FRITTERS

Students justify spending enormous amounts of time making up work schedules. These can be done for the day, evening, week, or whatever the relevant work session to be planned. Plans can be made not just for the coming work, but also for coming work breaks. Fritters of the future become bound into a longer series of work intentions and are in that way neutralized. Of course, scheduling may be resorted to whenever the actual progress of the work falls far enough off schedule to warrant the writing of a new one. Schedule-related fritters, then, become a consideration whenever something goes wrong or could go wrong with the schedule. Indeed, the more detailed the schedule, the greater the chance of derailment.

There are two salient forms of scheduling fritters. First, there are anticipated interruption fritters. If one knows in advance that at a certain point in the work period, studying will be interrupted by some other activity, there is set up a situation in which frittering the time until after the interruption is justified. This can be considered the application of a great divide fritter on a smaller scale. Second, there are disruption-of-sequence fritters. These occur whenever the student, for some reason, performs a task out of order from the planned sequence. If this involves successful completion of the different task, conditions are set up for an owe-it-to-yourself fritter as well as a new scheduling fritter. The disruption of sequence can also justify waiting for a new prominent starting point, like a new day, before actually working.

DEADLINE CHANGE FRITTERS

On occasion a teacher will change the date that some work is due either for the whole class or, by special arrangement, for single students. When this happens, the student feels free to use a postponed-deadline fritter. Since study time is reckoned backward from a deadline date rather than forward to new work opportunities, when the deadline is postponed, time is freed to avoid working. If, for example, a paper due Friday is postponed for one week on Wednesday, the student can wait for the following Wednesday before working again.

Preparation-Related Fritters

Preparation fritters involve all activities immediately attend-ant to preparing to study: getting books, paper, pens, cleaning the desk, and what have you. These are easily justified activities, preparatory as they are to work. These immediate preparations are easily escalated. Thus, a student decides that, in the interest of greater efficiency, he should clean his desk top (no matter what the actual nature of his work habits—tidy or abominable). Having done this, a crucial point is reached. He can now actually start to work. Instead, he says while-I'm-at-it and proceeds to clean out the whole desk, or rearrange all his books, or even move on to cleaning the whole room or apartment. This technique is especially interesting, developing as it does from the preparation fritter, in that it quickly ignores the originally work-related starting point. A good job is worth doing well, as long as it isn't the good job you have to do.

Preparation can be difficult (or made difficult), and work can be delayed. In the spread-resources or shuttle fritter the student does not bring, or chooses work for which he cannot bring, all the needed materials to one place for work. Travelling between work sites becomes necessary. What started as the path to work intersects with other paths (perhaps to other places).

Creativity Fritters

Once all the material preparations have been completed there are two other factors left to be prepared—the student and, say, the paper. Let us consider these in reverse order. Preparation of the paper itself will offer many opportunities for work avoidance.

(1) For the-first-step-is-the-hardest. This can mean working for a long time on an outline or, commonly, working hard at getting exactly the proper first sentence or first paragraph. The opening of a paper is felt in an important way to constrain the range of alternatives, stylistic and organizational, for the rest of the work. It becomes, therefore, of utmost importance that the opening be precisely correct—no matter how much time it takes.

(2) In addition, the student must be ready to work. Every creative endeavor, however, has an incubation period and every endeavor, creative or not, requires motivation. Both needs can require time, justified time. It is best to wait until you are bursting with ideas or are sufficiently motivated, even if the

motivation is guilt due to unsuccessful previous application of fritter techniques. This is therefore the let-it-brew-for-a-while fritter (closely related to this is the I'll-lie-down-and-think-about-it fritter; the possible danger in this tactic is, of course, very clear; listing all things people are designed to do horizontally, studying is one of the lowest on the list).

(3) Related to these is the I'm-sure-there-is-something-else fritter. No matter how much advanced preparation there has already been, the conscientious student is justified in allowing some free time to think of something else which should be included (say, in a paper, or when considering how to psych out the teacher's exam questions). This is especially useful when, for example, a paper is on a topic requiring an interdisciplinary approach or a number of different viewpoints for elucidation. The "something else" can then be in an area only vaguely related to the original topic. This justification can thus successfully be used to allow additional time for readings and thinking more and more peripheral to the original topic—i.e., to the work itself. When the task is taking a test, students can spend a great deal of time trying to psych out the teacher. Information on prior exams and teachers' specialization or personal quirks may be important in deciding what significant knowledge is.

Task-Involved Fritters

Finally, the student, to remain in concept and in fact a student, must occasionally actually work. Once work is started, however, there are still some devices which can be used to slow it or end it quickly without endangering one's view of self as student.

(1) One important consideration, especially to someone who has been using scheduling fritters, is a reliable measure of how quickly the work is going. Time is thus justifiably spent computing pages, hours, words per minute, or what have you. This is the what's-my-rate fritter.

(2) Every work goal can be divided into subgoals whose individual accomplishments are significant since each contributes to the final completion. This is the principle behind the logical-stop-

ping-point fritter. Small owe-it-to-yourself fritters are justified by the completion of the subgoals. As the time symmetry fritter has prominent dividing points for the time continuum, so the logical-stopping-point fritter divides up the work task itself. Thus, for example, one may set up subgoals such that one is justified in taking a break after completing only a single chapter in an assigned book. This technique, however, like the time symmetry fritter, is conducive to fractionalization. The subgoal can shift from finish the chapter to finish the topic of discussion or, more extremely, the page or the paragraph.

(3) Sometimes the student has more than one project to work on at once. The jack-of-all-trades fritter is a way of avoiding working too hard on any one subject by shifting from task to task before the work gets too taxing in any one of them.

(4) The hard-working student occasionally reaches a difficult place in his work. Work may slow down in the face of difficulty and require intense concentration. Overinvolvement, overconcern, and improper distance from the work may create problems. The student can then choose from a wide variety of more proper, and comfortable, distances from the work.

(5) As a result of using other fritter strategies, the working student may find the work cannot be done as desired in the remaining time before its deadline. It is possible to do an incredible-shrinking-work fritter. This allows a "settling process" to take place in which the wheat is separated from what becomes chaff.

Recovery Fritters

Sometimes the student does not complete the task when it is due. If he can get an open-ended extension, he is free to postpone additional work for a long time. This is the effect of the you-can't-pick-up-spilled-milk fritter.

FRITTERS AND GUILT

This presentation has been silent as to why fritters are successful in getting their work (avoiding work) done. It is clear how the time is frittered away, but it is not yet very clear how the student staves off guilt. Some suggestions of the mechanisms follow.

Many fritters deny that work performances are not being done as they should. A large number of fritters, especially task-related ones, disguise themselves as ways to get the task done. They either facilitate work (e.g., preparation), promise to improve it (e.g., related areas), or look like work (e.g., jack-of-all-trades). Biological necessity is sometimes seen as needed to get the task done, though occasionally this is a justification in its own right. Alternately, fritters can deny that there should be any pressure felt for not working. On one hand, the past shows no danger (prior capability, successful past work avoidance); on the other, there are no real consequences of not working (a form of what-the-hell sort. . . .).

Other fritters turn the fritterer's attention to other values above the successful study. These put the student role in larger perspective (alternate values) or put work in limits of "propriety" (appeals to fairness, "reasonable work" definitions).

Some fritters place special conditions on the way that work is done. Certain times to start (time symmetry), times to make progress (great-divide, anticipated-interruption), and times and places to stop (logical-stopping-point) are used to structure work sessions.

Finally, fritters can neutralize work pressure by subtle (or not so subtle) changes in how the definition of work is made. Is work "really" make work (one form of what-the-hell . . .), doing better than others (social-comparison), for posterity or your proctor (involved in pysch-out fritters), work you do or work due (postponed-deadline), a magnum opus or just some work (incredible-shrinking work)?

CONCLUDING REMARKS

Elements of the above presentation of fritter strategies lend themself readily to further research. Different fritters are used for different kinds of work. They are offerable as accounts to different others. Different others are needed to invoke particular fritters. Different fritters are used at different points in the phases of a work act. Different fritters are more subjectively available in different places, as, for example, the number of work cues varies by setting, requiring different fritter strategies. A student's cleaning the entire library before settling down to work would be rare. Some fritters are used without social support; others are not. Different materials are needed to use different fritters. Different fritters are used by students at different stages in their academic careers. Conditions which facilitate the adopting of different particular strategies must be elaborated. There is no evidence available yet on whether there are different subcultures of fritter or if these justifications are common currency among students in general. Because they are accounts to self which are only sometimes offered to others, students are often surprised when discussion reveals how widespread is their use.

There are features of the student role which facilitate the use of these strategies. Students are granted great liberty in the planning of their use of time. Student time is more often "individual time" than "social time." Time demands are stricter in high schools than in colleges. Required class time and daily evaluated assignments are less characteristic of the college years. The schools frequently cite the increased maturity of the students as the reason for the greater liberty permitted. However, time use in statuses occupied by even more mature adults are frequently more regulated by institutions. Perhaps most important, the student is in a transitional role. The schools and the population as a whole are not favorably disposed to lifetime students. It is an early stage in commitment to professional careers and a late stage in formal education for yet other careers. Widespread use of fritter techniques can ease the difficulties of early commitment for the former and aid the termination of formal education for the latter.

REFERENCES

MATZA, D. (1964) Delinquency and Drift. New York: John Wiley.
SCOTT, M. and S. LYMAN (1970) "Accounts, deviance and social order," pp. 89-119 in J. D. Douglas (ed.) Deviance and Respectability. New York: Basic Books.
––– (1968) "Accounts." Amer. Soc. Rev. 33, 1: 46-62.

LYN H. LOFLAND's major research interests are in the social psychology of urban life. An Assistant Professor of Sociology at the University of California, Davis, she taught previously at the University of California, Berkeley, and earned her Ph.D. at the University of California, San Francisco.

SELF-MANAGEMENT IN PUBLIC SETTINGS:

LYN HEBERT LOFLAND

THE PERIOD OF APPROACH is a very brief one. While it is in process, the individual is primarily concerned with projecting himself only as someone who can successfully execute this maneuver. There is time for little else. It is not until after he has reached a position and is faced with a prolonged stay in the midst of strangers that it becomes important—or even possible—for him to assume his more individualistic and complex management style. His overriding concern continues to be that of projecting a favorable and confirmable image, but with more time now at his disposal, this projection will involve a greater range of behavior and will reflect more individual differences than was possible during the approach.

AUTHOR'S NOTE: For a more detailed discussion of these and other matters, see my new book, *A World of Strangers: Order and Action in Urban Public Space,* forthcoming from Basic Books in the spring of 1973.

EDITOR'S NOTE: Part I of this article, appearing in URBAN LIFE, I, 1, suggested that the public places of cities, as the loci of contacts among heterogeneous strangers, do not provide the conditions for "self"-support, esteem, and protection that make social life bearable and possible. As such, cities, or more

In the Midst of Strangers: Management Styles

While management styles differ among different individuals, their range is not infinite, and it is possible to observe some main patterns or types. We shall look at five of these (or more precisely, four, plus a category of persons who seem to lack them altogether—the mavericks). The order of their presentation is based upon the amount of presentation "relaxation" or behavioral expression each style allows—from the most to the least restricted. The degree of each style's restrictiveness, I want to suggest, is a function of the extent to which the person exhibiting the style perceives the setting as more or less dangerous and himself in more or less need of protection. We begin with the most restricted, and thus most protective style—that of the "sweet young thing"—and end with the style that is so unrestricted and so unprotective as to be no style at all—that of the "maverick."[1]

THE SWEET YOUNG THING

The most restricted and protective of management styles is used primarily, as the name suggests, by females, ranging in age from late teens to mid-thirties. That the female urbanite should feel a need for the most protective style is understandable. Women in American society are thought to be subject to sexual advances in public settings and girls are taught from an early age to beware of strange men. Our folk tales abound with stories of

---

specifically, their public sectors, were said to be dangerous. It was suggested further that much public behavior might usefully be viewed as the expression of various strategies for coping with the specific problems generated by this danger. The problem of *entering* a stranger-filled setting was considered and a number of coping techniques were described.

We shall now go on to consider the problem of *remaining* in a setting for a period of time and look closely at various management styles utilized by persons who must do so. A final section will analyze the relations between strangers in public settings more generally and will view them as involving a "bargain" vis-à-vis the conditions under which stranger selves will be supported.

dangers that may befall the woman alone. Young women particularly, as the most prized of sexual objects and the most inexperienced in the ways of "city life," are thought to be in greatest peril.

The style of the "Sweet Young Thing" involves very little movement. Having once taken a position, usually a seated one, she rarely leaves it. Her posture is straight; potentially suggestive or revealing "slouching" is not dared. She crosses her legs or her ankles, but takes great care to see that no more of her is showing than current standards of good taste allow.

She inevitably has a book or magazine in her possession, and this is drawn from her coat or handbag the moment she has settled herself in a position. The book or magazine is never closely read; to become engrossed is to risk losing awareness and control of one's posture. In addition, it is essential to be on a constant lookout for any approaching danger. But while reading material receives little close attention, it is always conspicuously present, either lying on the lap or held out from the body with one hand, about midway between the lap and the face. Such a prop serves to demonstrate that she is tending to her own affairs, not on the prowl for strange males and not the type of young lady who would invite attention by boldly staring about. While she does gaze at her surroundings, her glances are usually short and casual, risking no eye contact. On the occasions when she allows herself to simply stare, she makes certain her eyes are turned toward the floor, chair, wall, potted plant, or any other inanimate object.

Should the occasion arise when she must leave her position and move to another location, she does so purposefully, in a businesslike, no-nonsense way. She does not "stroll" from one part of the setting to another. Having first carefully planned her move, she proceeds with all deliberate speed to her new destination.

THE NESTER

The "Nester" style derives its name from the main activity

engaged in by those who use it. Having once established a position, such persons busy themselves with arranging and rearranging their "props," much in the manner of a bird building and occupying a nest. Nesters in public settings are possessed of an amazing number of items of personal property and they spend most of their time in the setting caring for them. They are primarily young men and middle-aged women and, whatever the sex, they are always very neat in appearance.

The Nester is somewhat less restricted in his movements than is the Sweet Young Thing, although like her, having once secured a position, he rarely leaves it. Indeed, he is really much too busy to do so. However, unlike the Sweet Young Thing, the Nester is not confined to one rigid posture. In fact, his duties require that he have considerable freedom of body movement within the confines of his position.

Sometimes the Nester's possessions, though numerous, are small in size, as is the case with the young man described below who was able to carry them all in his pocket, a small briefcase, and a paper sack.

A young man, mid-twenties, sits down on one of the benches in the bus depot. He places a briefcase, which he had carried under his arm, on his lap and opens it. He withdraws several small pieces of paper, examining each with some intensity, then returns them to the case. He stands up slightly so as to pull some coins from his pants pocket, then sits again and counts the money several times before returning it to the pocket. Now he takes a check book from the brief case and spends a few minutes bringing the check register up to date. The checkbook is returned to the case and a spiral notebook is withdrawn. He begins writing, but this too lasts only a few minutes. Then the notebook is replaced, the briefcase closed, and a paper sack is set neatly on top of it. In a few seconds, the paper sack is removed, the briefcase reopened and a packet of letter-sized paper is withdrawn. He glances through these, returns them, and then in rapid succession, pulls out and returns a newspaper, book, brochure, and letter-size envelope.

On other occasions, the Nester may be kept busy looking

after items of a much bulkier nature. In such cases, there is a good deal more standing up and sitting down, lifting and juggling, than in the situation illustrated above. Witness the activity of a middle-class woman in her late forties or early fifties.

> A yellow convertible stops outside the bus depot and a woman emerges. She makes several trips from the car to the locker area, finally places a number of items in one of the lockers and leaves. About a half hour later, she returns, her arms laden with additional packages. She sets them on a bench, goes to the lockers, retrieves what has been placed inside and brings these things to the bench as well. Her possessions now include two dress boxes, a hat box, a suitcase, a purse, a paper sack, and a raincoat on a hanger, protected by a plastic cover. She sits down next to this stack and begins to arrange them. The suitcase is placed on the floor, dress boxes on top, the raincoat is laid across the back of the bench. Her purse and the paper sack are placed next to her. She surveys this handiwork and, apparently dissatisfied, begins to rearrange it. This arranging and rearranging continues for fifteen minutes until a bus is called and she transports all her gear, in several trips, out to the loading area.

Should the Nester be required to forsake his position temporarily, he does so only after making certain that everything is in place (if he cannot take it all with him). Even if he must leave some things behind, he does not move to his new destination empty-handed, but carries some item, such as a briefcase, with him. During the passage, he continues his work, looking through or tidying up whatever item he was able to bring along. Once returned to the initial position, he inevitably finds that the props left behind need to be rearranged once more.

This absorption with props functions to increase the Nester's protection. First, it keeps his eyes occupied so that he does not have to be concerned with eye contact (a type of contact which strangers often take great pains to avoid). Second, his busyness suggests to those around him that here is a person who has many important things to do and is therefore not a person with whom one should attempt any verbal interaction. Under some conditions, interaction between strangers in public settings is both legitimate and commonplace. But the Nester, apparently wishing to avoid all interaction, legitimate or not, presents himself so as to discourage any interactional opening.

THE INVESTIGATOR

Less confining in body movement than either of the previous styles, the Investigator stance nevertheless protects those who utilize it from eye contact and undesired interaction. Investigators, (primarily mature—late thirties or older males) are quite as absorbed and thus as unapproachable as Nesters. But, unlike Nesters, the objects of their absorption are not personal "props" but the various facilities of the setting itself.

Having first reached a position, the Investigator surveys his surroundings with some care. Then, having done this, he leaves his position to begin a minute investigation of every inanimate object in sight. Occasionally he returns to his initial position or establishes a new one, but most of his time is spent moving about. The Investigator is at his best, of course, if the setting is large and complex and presents a wide array of items for him to look at. But if the setting contains no such "lush growth," he remains undaunted. A truly skilled Investigator can spend five minutes gazing at a sign which contains only three words. Let us follow one Investigator as he moves about a small but well-supplied bus depot.

A middle- or lower-middle-class male, early forties, is wandering about. He spends a few moments standing in front of a small-gift vending machine, looking at the display of available items, then sits down on the bench across from the machine to continue his investigation. He rises, goes up the stairs to the restroom, stopping en route to look at the various signs which adorn the walls. Leaving the restroom, he moves to the front of the depot, taking note of the menus on the wall behind the lunch counter. Now he comes further into the depot again, stops in front of a medal-making machine and proceeds to read all the instructions printed on it. He comes back even further, now gazes at a sign urging travelers to tag their luggage. Leaving this spot, he moves to a Diners Club display—a desk-like arrangement with a sign asking people to fill out applications for a Diners Club card. There is a place on the desk apparently designed to hold applications, but it is empty. He remains in front of the desk for about three minutes, then goes back to the gift machine which once again receives his studied attention. Now he goes out the side exit and looks at the buses parked in the runway, comes back in, stands gazing out the window to the runway. Leaving this location, he goes to the rear exit, looks out at the parking lot for some five minutes. Coming back into the middle of the depot, he examines a coke machine and the photo booth situated next to it; then sits down at the bench facing these two items and continues his examination. He rises after a few minutes and goes over to the phone booths, spends about four minutes looking through the telephone directory.

The Investigator will continue this kind of movement during the entire time he is in the setting. When he leaves he will have given a few moments of undivided attention to every machine, phone booth, sign, clock, window, door, chair, ash tray, water fountain, and newspaper stand in the place.

THE SEASONED URBANITE

Of the conventional or nondeviant management styles, that of the Seasoned Urbanite is the least restricted and thus least protective. It appears to be used, as might be expected, primarily by persons who by reason of age or long experience in public settings, feel they have little to fear.

The Seasoned Urbanite may be either male or female. If male, he tends to be in his late forties or fifties, if female, somewhat older.

The Seasoned Urbanite is confined to no fixed position, body posture, or task involvement. Should he be reading, he does so as though truly engrossed, settling himself comfortably in his chair, often sliding down, spreading his legs out before him and resting his head against the chair back. He may involve himself with personal props, but for shorter periods of time and with less absorption than does the Nester. He moves about the setting easily, may glance at the various signs or displays, but with considerably less interest than is shown by the Investigator.

The main protections of the Seasoned Urbanite appear to be age which, particularly for females, reduces the chances for any sexual advances; and long experience in public settings which assures him of the knowledge and skills necessary to handle any difficulties. Seasoned Urbanites, particularly females, frequently open themselves to verbal interaction with strangers, secure in their ability to judge others accurately on the basis of body presentation and body language alone.

THE MAVERICK

This final management style is actually a nonstyle, and its users are those who either do not know how, are not able, or do not care to protect themselves in public settings. Mavericks are likely to draw what for conventional others would be considered threatening attention; they make spectacles of themselves as persons who possess inadequate, unworthy, or illegitimate selves. Those who observe them, disturbed by their apparent lack of respect for proper presentation, avoid them as much as possible; but Mavericks do not play by the rules and will often force themselves into interaction with unwilling strangers.

There are three types of persons who may be said to be Mavericks: *children,* or those with insufficiently developed selves; *the constantly stigmatized,* or those with "spoiled" selves (e.g., those afflicted with cerebral palsy or other diseases affecting the capacity to discipline body movements); and *eccentrics,* or those with "irresponsible" selves. Of these, we shall consider only the last.

The *eccentric* fails to present a proper management style presumably because he is too preoccupied with his own thoughts to be aware that one is required. As such, eccentrics present a particular problem to conventional others. They are so unconcerned with or insensitive to the responses of others that they are immune to sanctions which might socialize them, as with children; or to sanctions which might shame them, as with the constantly stigmatized.

Eccentrics show no concern for body presentation, appearing in public in the most outlandish of outfits. Nor do they appear concerned that their behavior may attract undue attention. They often misuse the setting quite openly and without any apparent awareness that they are doing so. Since they are unresponsive to sanctions, they are unpredictable and present a greater threat to the protection of the self than does any other stranger in a public setting. We shall be meeting a number of eccentrics in the following section, for it is in the relation between them and more conventional types that the "public bargain" is most clearly exposed. For now, a single example will suffice to acquaint the reader with the eccentric's style—or lack of it.

A very tall young male enters a bus depot. He is bearded, his hair is dark and long and rather kinky and it seems to stick out in all directions. He is wearing a green wool "logger" shirt, with a white shirt beneath it and wool slacks in a gray plaid design. He is moving all around the depot with great speed, rushing from one section to another, as though he had a specific destination in mind and were in a great hurry to reach it. He goes to the water fountain, then to the Diners Club display, back to the water fountain, takes a drink, turns on his heels, heads up toward the restrooms three stairs at a time. Still rushing, he comes back down, out the side exit, back in and out the rear exit. A few seconds later he reappears, this time hurrying through the front door, comes all the way into the depot and out the side exit again. Again he reappears at the front entrance, rushes through the depot until he reaches a bench, plops down, leans back his head and heaves a loud sigh. Now up again and out the side exit, in the front door and back into the depot, reaches the side exit, whirls around, takes two steps away from the door, whirls again and goes out. Returns a second later through the same door, strides rapidly to the front, out the entrance and disappears.

THE PUBLIC BARGAIN, THE SOCIAL BARGAIN, AND URBAN PARADOX

In Part I of this article, it was suggested that social life may be viewed as a kind of social bargain, a whispered enjoinder to let us all protect each other so we can carry on the business of living. It was further suggested that while this bargain obtained among persons who knew one another, among strangers in an urban public setting, no such assurance of mutual protection was given.

This is not to say that persons in public settings do not support each other's selves. In fact, most persons in a public setting most of the time are doing just that. All the various tactics of self-management just discussed and many additional tactics which we have not considered are, in most instances, as protective to others in the setting as they are to persons utilizing them. And, on occasion, persons may help their fellow urbanites out of simple generosity. Nevertheless, mutual support and protection of each other's selves is not characteristic of the interaction between unknown others. Under only one set of circumstances will the urbanite in a public setting inevitably and invariably go out of his way to protect and support the self of the other; only under circumstances where to refuse the support would be to put himself in danger. Thus, the *public bargain* may be viewed as an agreement between strangers guaranteeing mutual "self"-support *only* under conditions where the failure to extend such support would prove dangeous to the one refusing it.

At first glance, there would seem to be a qualitative difference between the public and social bargains—the latter appears to be an expression of genuine human kindness, the former a mere expression of human self-centeredness. Perhaps, the critics are right—the "goodness" of humanity is lost in the city. But let us look more closely.

While mutual support and protection may be characteristic of the interaction between known others, it is by no means inevitable. There are many instances and circumstances in which we "put one another down," in which we challenge one another's selves, in which we even enjoy the other's discomfort elicited by our actions. Despite its frequency, such behavior is not the common coin of human interaction; if it were, social life, perhaps human life, as we know them would not be possible. Such behavior is not the common coin because we are all too much involved in each other. We cannot tear at the other too much because to do so is to threaten the meaning system which supports us both. That is, we agree to support each other because to fail to do so would be a threat to our selves.

The discerning reader will note that the circumstances just described under which the social bargain operates are identical to the circumstances described above under which the public bargain operates. They are, in effect, the same bargain. The difference between acquaintance interaction and stranger interaction lies primarily in the *frequency* with which circumstances conspire to make mutual protectiveness essential. When we are among persons whom we know, with whom our lives are intertwined, we can *avoid* mutual support only rarely. Among persons we do not know, and will undoubtably never see again, we need *provide* support only rarely.

Thus, it is legitimate to talk of a public bargain, as distinct from a social bargain, only because the circumstances which bring the former into operation are so limited. If the world of strangers is a more dangerous place than the world of acquaintances, it is not because the human is kind in one world and cruel in the other. It is, rather, because one world presents more instances in which self-preservation dictates kindness than does the other.

In the world of strangers, these instances are greatly delimited. What kinds of actions the public bargain will support depends on what kind of person is performing the action. With conventional humans, support is rarely required. But among Mavericks—those persons lacking the "decency" to have a protective management style—almost all contact is fraught with danger. The Maverick is so unpredictable that to challenge any of his actions in any way is to run the risk that his next action will lead to danger for the self.

All Mavericks represent constant threats to all others in the setting. However, unpredictable as they are, children may be controlled. They are small and, if necessary, force may be used to bring them into line. And the constantly stigmatized, despite their inability to control their bodies, are, after all, just like everyone else inside. It is understood that they would most certainly adopt a conventional management style if they could. But eccentrics are another matter altogether. Not only are they unpredictable, they are "irresponsible" and unresponsive to sanctions. Thus, it is in the urbanite's contact with eccentrics that we may observe the full fruition of the public bargain.

Once an individual has definitely established himself as an eccentric, he may engage in the most bizarre behavior without exciting the "slightest notice." Almost no matter how peculiar his appearance or how odd his actions, he will be treated as though he looked and acted like a conventional human being. Of course, should his behavior appear excessively bizarre or potentially physically dangerous, someone may call the authorities. But this is an action that is taken behind his back. To his face, the elaborate fiction of his complete "normality" will continue to be acted out.

At its most simple, the operation of the public bargain between urbanites and eccentrics may involve no more than disattention to peculiarities in presentation, as in thy following incident.

We entered the coffee shop about 11:00 p.m. and sat in booths along one side. I was sitting so that I could see everyone in the booths ahead of us, all the way up to the door. We had not been there very long when a man of about fifty came in and sat himself down about three booths ahead, facing in my direction. He ordered, and for awhile I did not pay much attention to him, that is, until a murmur of conversation and a slight blur of movement made me look again in his direction. There he sat, eating his dinner, and quite clearly carrying on an animated conversation with someone who, also quite clearly, was not there. This invisible companion, to judge by the man's actions, was apparently seated on the other side of the table. As time passed, the conversation became more audible, and the man began to gesture more boldly, apparently involved in some very intense conversation. His invisible companion carried on his part in the interchange, for every few minutes the man would stop, cock his head, hold his fork suspended, and listen in rapt attention to what his companion had to say. There were not very many people in the coffee shop, and those who were present were going out of their way to pretend they hadn't noticed. There was a young couple sitting in a booth right across the aisle from him and they were taking great pains to keep from looking at him and to stifle any laughter that might threaten to arise. I could see the employees every once in a while duck into a kitchen area to laugh quietly among themselves, or at least comment on the behavior, but I noted that the waitress who served the old gentlemen, did so with great calm, waiting patiently should he be in the midst of conversation, until he had finished before asking if he wanted anything else. Incidentally, the invisible companion apparently was not hungry, for no food was ordered for him. I'm not quite certain what would have happened had an order for two been placed, but I rather suspect that it would have been served without comment.

When eccentrics and urbanites are engaged in verbal contact, the successful operation of the bargain becomes a bit more complex. Here one must do more than simply keep one's eyes averted. One must communicate the normality fiction through facial expression, words, and body language. To fail to do so is to challenge the eccentric's self, and to do what is to risk all the dangers of unpredictability. In the following example, two "conventionals" are in interaction with an eccentric. One of the "conventionals" knows the eccentric slightly. To the other, she is a complete stranger. Note that during the time the eccentric is present, she receives full support from them both. Only after she has gone do they feel free to express their true feelings about her behavior.

A working-class woman, late forties or early fifties, is seated at one of the horseshoe counters in a large coffee shop in a bus depot. She is cleanly dressed, wearing a sweater and print dress. As she is drinking her coffee, a woman in her mid seventies comes out of an adjoining cafeteria and greets her. The newcomer is dressed in a rather motley collection of unmatched, apparently second-hand and terribly wrinkled and dirty items of apparel. Her dress is of a shiny satin-like material and is badly tattered. It hangs loosely around her as though it were several sizes too large. Over this, she wears a shiny, equally shapeless satin coat, apparently designed for wear on formal occasions. It contains a very large hole in one elbow. A badly bedraggled hat, with a tiara-like frame, is on her head. She is carrying a large paper shopping bag which appears to be almost full, although nothing within it is identifiable. The old woman stops beside her acquaintance. "Enjoying hot coffee, huh?" They exchange a few words. The old woman looks about her and notices that on the counter are several dirty, small paper plates, used by the coffee shop for serving sandwiches and pie. She picks up one nearest to her and asks her acquantance, "Do you think I can have it? They usually give them to me. I have a collection of them, you know." The acquaintance says nothing for at this point the waitress approaches them. The old woman asks the waitress if she may have the plate. The waitress nods, her face showing neither surprise nor puzzlement. Another plate further down the counter comes to the old lady's attention, but before she can reach it, the waitress has picked it up and placed it in the wastecan. Noticing this, the lady asks the waitress if she may have the second plate. Again the waitress remains expressionless, pulls it out from the trash and hands it to her. Noticing other plates in the wastecan, she asks if she might have those too, and in a short time she has all the dirty plates available in that section of the coffee shop in her possession. As she receives each one, she wipes it off slightly with a napkin and places it in her shopping bag. After she completes wiping off and packing the last plate, she bids good-bye to her acquaintance and disappears. A few moments later, the waitress approaches the other woman and asks her what the old lady does with all those paper plates. Her face is not expressionless now, and she quite clearly means to indicate that she thinks the now departed lady is a little crazy. The woman answers that she thinks the old lady has children to visit her and uses the plates, after cleaning them up, to serve refreshments to her visitors. Having verbalized this explanation, she apparently finds it unsatisfactory even to herself, shrugs her shoulders and laughs, and says to the waitress: "I don't really know exactly what she does with them." The two women exchange knowing smiles and the interaction between them ends.

There is a marvelous paradox in all this. The conventional, striving desperately to always appear as an adequate, worthy, and legitimate human being, often need make only the slightest error to lose support for and confirmation of his desired image of self. But the eccentric, whose every action, whose very appearance, constitutes an error, is granted support and confirmation almost no matter what he does. The most dangerous opponent in the great urban world of danger is the most carefully protected from harm.

NOTE

1. These five are not exhaustive of the full range of possibilities. They are largely based on observations of people in non-task-oriented settings, specifically, waiting settings. Such a basis is selective and less than representative. This type of setting, however, has its advantages. The setting itself places only broad, general restrictions on how the waiting time may be spent. There is considerable opportunity, therefore, for individual styles to be expressed *and* observed. While it seems quite likely that persons in theatres, for example, exhibit differences in how they handle self-presentation (through sitting postures, gestures, and the like), the highly specific task-oriented character of such settings restricts both the extent to which such differences may be expressed and the ease with which they may be observed. A waiting area, on the other hand, is a kind of "fishbowl" in which management styles obscured in other settings may operate fully and be seen clearly.

II. SUBORDINATION

Subordination as a social situation is a point of view for thinking about social life and organizing experience rather than an exhaustive way of characterizing the total life-situation of any individual, or very many individuals, at least. For subordinates may also be superordinates in the same situation at different times or in other situations, as when subordinate workers go home to be family superordinates. The three studies appearing here point up, moreover, the deliciously generic and omnitopical character of subordination. It is omni-institutional and all-pervasive, found obviously in courts (Coleman), clearly in occupations (Bigus), and lurking even and less obviously at the doorway (Walum).

LAUREL RICHARDSON WALUM is an Assistant Professor of Sociology at The Ohio State University. She engages in teaching and research in sociological theory, political-sociology, and gender-roles.

THE CHANGING DOOR CEREMONY:

Notes on the Operation of Sex Roles

in Everyday Life

LAUREL RICHARDSON WALUM

A YOUNG WOMAN AND A YOUNG MAN, total strangers to each other, simultaneously reach the closed classroom door. She steps slightly aside, stops, and waits. He positions himself, twists the handle, pulls open the door and holds it while she enters. Once she is safely across the threshold, he enters behind her. An everyday, commonplace social ceremony has been performed. It is not accidental that their performance in this ceremonial ritual of "door-opening" has gone so smoothly, although they have never rehearsed it with each other. Nor is it by chance that such trivial, commonplace ceremonies between the sexes occur day after day.

Of the multitude of such ceremonial occasions between the sexes in middle-class society—occasions wherein the interplay of cultural values and self-image are displayed—the "Door Ceremony" is probably the most common. We are confronted constantly with doors: car doors, house doors, bathroom doors, revolving doors, electric eye doors. Ad infinitum are the physical structures which must somehow be penetrated if we are to complete our daily round of activities. And nearly as often as we confront the door, we are in a social situation in which a ceremonial ritual concerning it may occur. The pervasiveness of the occasion is difficult to deny. The relevance of the ceremony for the maintenance of cultural values and self esteem, its true *non-triviality,* was initially suggested to me by entries in student journals—the journals having been written for a Sociology of Women course. It was subsequently underscored by a series of norm violation experiments performed by undergraduates and by my own observation. I draw my illustration and develop my analysis from these data sources.

I am concerned with four major questions: (1) How does this ceremony function to bind the society together? (2) What cultural values are being enacted? (3) What consequences has the women's movement had on the ceremony? and finally, speculatively (4) What might the future hold?

Goffman has paid special attention to these ceremonial occasions. In our everyday associations we abide by rules of conduct, a kind of guide book which is followed "not because it is pleasant, cheap or effective, but because it is suitable and just" (1967: 48). These rules establish both our obligations—the way we are morally constrained to act, and our expectations— the way others are morally required to act towards us. Commitment to the rule becomes a commitment to a given self-image. Ceremonial rules guide

> conduct in matters felt to have secondary importance—officially anyway—as a conventionalized means of communication by which the individual expresses his character or conveys his appreciation of other participants in the situation [Goffman 1967: 54].

These rules are incorporated in what we call "etiquette." To be properly mannered we convey an appropriate demeanor, expressed through our dress, deportment, bearing, and an appropriate deference, or appreciation and confirmation of an actor's relationship to a recipient.

The rules of conduct bind actors and recipients in appropriate interaction, encourage their interaction, and serve in a daily pedestrian way to hold together the social order. The very dailiness of the ceremonies, the lack of substantive investment, permits the constant reaffirmation of the kinds of persons we think we are and the kinds of rules we deem appropriate. The ceremony, then, affirms the nature of the social order, the morality of it, as well as the properness of the self who is engaged in the action. As Goffman succinctly states, "The gestures which we sometimes call empty are perhaps, in fact, the fullest things of all" (1967: 91).

BINDING THE SOCIETY

The Door Ceremony exemplifies the etiquette developed to "bind" the sexes together. The daily drama of Betty Co-ed and Joe College at the Classroom Door, which began this analysis, is descriptive of the usual ritual. Joe College, under the ceremonial rules of conduct, is *obliged* to open the door for Betty Co-ed, and Betty Co-ed *expects* to be the recipient of his courtesy. In the ritual, both of them have confirmed their images of themselves as respectively, male and female. As one "Joe College" wrote in his course journal.

> I have dated several girls including my fiancée who want to be treated like a lady. My courtesy like opening the car door makes them feel more feminine and they enjoy this. I enjoy also being a gentleman and making them feel this way. Personally, I prefer a girl who is feminine over a more rugged-looking and -acting girl.

And as a Betty Co-ed declared:

> Tonight I had a date with a gentleman. When I opened the door to let myself in, he closed it and opened it again. To tell the truth it made me feel good. He said he enjoyed doing these little things for me because he derived a feeling of protectiveness. I was reassured. I

didn't want him to think I was crude. It's nice to *feel* like a woman.

The activity as traditionally structured, then, affirms the generalized notion of "masculinity" and "femininity." But what are the components, the elements, of the personal self-image enacted in the door ceremony that lead the male to perceive himself as "masculine," and the female to see herself as "feminine?"

To be masculine, first and foremost, means to have authority, to be in charge, in control. And in our culture, in most encounters, the person with higher authority holds the door. The doctor ushers in his patient, the mother—her children, the Dean—his faculty, and the young and able facilitate the old and infirm. Note that the phrase, the "gate-keepers of knowledge," symbolically acknowledges the role of authority vested in those responsible for the door.

Secondly, and pervasively, to be "masculine" means to be "active;" to be "feminine" means to be "passive." This distinction pervades the entire ceremony. The male is the active party in the encounter; the female waits passively for the door to open and for the door to close. The passivity is closely linked to another prescribed feminine trait, namely "dependence." By waiting for the service to be performed, the woman communicates that she *needs* someone to help her through her daily round of activities. The male, in turn, communicates his independence by actively meeting the challenge of the door and overcoming it. Other male virtues of physical strength, mechanical ability, worldliness, self-confidence, and efficacy are called into play in the ceremony. If Joe College goes through his routine without mishap, he has engaged all these traits culturally associated with masculinity, and of course, he does *feel* masculine. And Betty Co-ed, by acting out her expectations, has drawn upon the perceptions of femininity recognized by the culture: fraility, weakness, ineptitude and protectibility. She *feels* womanly.

AFFIRMATION OF CULTURAL VALUES

The door ceremony, then, reaffirms for both sexes their sense of gender-identity, of being a "masculine" or "feminine" person. It is not accidentally structured. In a very profound way the simple ceremony daily makes a reality of the moral perspective of their culture: the *ideology of patriarchy*. These virtues of "masculinity" are precisely those which are the dominant values of the culture: aggression, efficacy, authority, prowess, and independence. And these virtues are assigned to the dominant group, the males (cf. Millet, 1970: 23-58). Opening a door for a woman, presumably only a simple, common courtesy, is also a *political* act, an act which affirms a patriarchal ideology. The male who wrote the following recognized not the irony of his words.

> Some women feel that if you open a door for them it is a sign of male chauvinism. In other words, you can't be nice to a female without showing your true colors.

His words, however, are perhaps less naive than this more commonly heard statement.

> I'm all for Woman's Lib. I think women should get equal pay for equal work. But women should keep their femininity. I like being treated like a lady.

One might suggest that these people are missing the relevance of minor courtesies perpetuating the ideology of patriarchy. Analytically, in terms of our understandings of the relationship between the cultural values and everyday ceremonies, women can't have it both ways.

EFFECTS OF THE WOMAN'S MOVEMENT

As more and more women and men "recognize" the meaning that common courtesies have for the perpetuation of the patriarchal ideology, increasing numbers of what Goffman refers to as deference confrontations occur. The world which has been taken for granted, the rules of conduct once abided by, are called into question. Ceremonial rituals, once performed with propriety, become imbued with substantive meaning and are perceived by some as insulting, assaulting, and degrading. As a consequence, the once routine—matter-of-fact—door-opening ceremony becomes situationally problematic to increasing numbers of people. What are some of the responses to the altered consciousness? What stances do persons take to make sense out of their changed ceremonial world? I offer a kind of typology of such stances based on empirical observations and student reports. I do not claim that it is an exhaustive theoretical accounting, but, rather, only an analytical categorization of known patterns.

1. The Confused

Many persons confronted for the first time with a ceremonial profanation are uncertain what to do about it. They have practiced the standard behaviors and do not know how to respond when one of the actors is out of "character." A woman reports the following:

> I approached a door ahead of a fellow and then with common courtesy, I held it open for him to go through. He bumped right into me even though he could see me. He looked awfully puzzled and it took him forever to get through.

The "confused" man could indeed see her but he could not perceive what was "happening" and was unable to make sense out of it. He acted along his normal path—destined for collision. Confusion is even more explicit in another reported episode.

> I came to a door at the same time as this guy. He reached to open it for me but then I started to open it myself and he just let me do it. *It was like neither of us knew what to do.*

The Confused, embarrassed and awkward, literally don't know yet, how to make sense out of the situation.

2. The Tester

The Tester, unlike the Confused, *recognizes* that the routine rules of conduct in any given encounter are violatable, and yet wants to maintain proper demeanor as well as proper deference. For example, a woman reports that "A man opening a door holds it open for me, asking, 'Are you a liberated woman? If not, I'll hold this door open for you.' " Or, take, the following overheard conversation.

Female: Well, aren't you going to open the door for me?

Male: I didn't know that girls still like for boys to do that.

Female: I'm not in Woman's Lib.

Often, the Tester has other motives in mind, such as wanting to act properly in order to "score." This excerpt from a male student's journal is illustrative.

It's almost like discovering a third sex to deal with liberated women. In the past I would make advances to my date almost as a matter of course. Now, I must "discover" if my date is sexually traditional or not before I decide on the conduct of our date. I can't just open doors and light cigarettes and expect to score. In fact, if I do treat those so-called "liberated" women like chattels, we never make it.

This male has found, then, that the whole course of his sexual life can hinge on the perception of appropriate deference.

3. The Humanitarian

The Humanitarian, like the Tester, recognizes that the situation is changing but has drawn upon other cultural values to explain and guide behavior, particularly the values of "sensitivity" and of "considerateness" of all people. For example, one male states,

> A male shouldn't *circle* the car to open the door for a woman. I believe each sex should treat the other with mutual courtesy. If a woman reaches the car first, there is nothing wrong with her opening it.

Or, as another male student writes,

> I had a 15 second encounter with a pro-libber which has left a bad taste in my mouth all day. She had a large stack of papers and I pushed open and held the door for her. I would have done this for a woman or a man. Instead of thank you I got the coldest, bitterest, most glaring stare that went right through me. I resent being seen as a Pig when I was being courteous to her as a *person*.

There are women humanitarians, also, who open doors for men in similar straits. As one reports,

> I entered the elevator ahead of a football player who lives in my building who had an armful of groceries. I quickly held the door back so he could get on. He was so embarrassed he couldn't even say thank-you.

4. The Defender

The Defender recognizes there is change afoot in the land but wants no part of it. For example, one woman relates:

> I opened a door to enter a building and a boy walked in ahead of me. It was just like he expected me to open the door for him. My first reaction was frowning and thinking some people have a lot of nerve. I believe in manners that did not enter the mind of the boy. I wondered if most boys now take it for granted that girls are woman's liberationists and will want to hold the door open for boys.

And a male student observes:

It happens many times in this University that the female *purpose-fully* beats the male to the door and opens it herself. To the male, this is a discourtesy and an example of bad manners. To him it appears that the female is a hard and calloused woman who has never been taught proper manners. They are trying to assert their person over their sex.

Another male student concluded a multi-paragraph moral indictment of "lady door-openers" with this clincher: "It's fine that women are liberating themselves, but I wouldn't want to marry one." The vehemence of Defenders occasionally creates poignant episodes, as evidenced by this journal entry.

"I don't care how uncomfortable you are. You are not going until you act like my wife should," my husband stormed. I conceded. I let him open the car door. I had to give in. I don't have a driving license.

5. The Rebel

The Rebel recognizes that the rules of conduct are changing and is anxious to speed the change on its way. Rebels are oftimes involved in badly demeanored profanations and report pleasure in their sacrilege. One woman states,

I had a date with this same fellow [previously referred to as a gentleman] and this time I *deliberately* opened the door. He looked distressed. So I rubbed it in and told him I was capable of opening the door myself. I never wanted to go out with him in the first place. Ha!

Another woman student reports:

So this Dude says to me, "Hey, let me help you with the door." And I say, "You ain't got nothin' to help me with."

Males appear also in the Rebel ranks. Says one,

I don't open doors for women. I'm glad not to. I don't want to serve them just because they're women. If they had their heads screwed on right they wouldn't trade doing laundry for me lighting their cigarettes.

WHAT THE FUTURE HOLDS

As is obvious from the illustrations, these five types are in frequent interaction with each other, making the ceremonial occasion increasingly complex and non-routine. Where do we go from here? Can we expect to get through those doors? Durkheim and Goffman argue that the social order is dependent on the routine daily acting-out of the morality of people who are simultaneously being bound together and providing living testimony of the cultural values. If altered consciousness continues and courtesies are rebuked, then ceremonial profanations will increase in frequency. The increase in violations of rules of conduct leads to increasing normlessness—anomie. The anomic period provides a time for the emergence of new *substantive* rules of conduct. A potential substantive change, then, might be forthcoming. If patriarchal values, which now govern the ceremonial conduct between the sexes, cannot be routinely enacted, these values cannot persist. Looking to changing values in other realms, and speaking optimistically, we might even be able to foresee ceremonial occasions dominated by a humanitarian perspective. If so, we might all get through our daily rounds with increased efficacy and joy.

REFERENCES

GOFFMAN, E. (1967) "The nature of deference and demeanor," pp. 47-96 in Interaction Ritual: Essays on Face-to-Face Behavior. Garden City, N.Y.: Doubleday Anchor.
MILLETT, K. (1970) Sexual Politics. Garden City, N.Y.: Doubleday.

RONALD V. COLEMAN earned a B.A. in Sociology at the University of
California, Davis in 1975 and is currently traveling and working in several parts
of North America.

COURT CONTROL

AND GRIEVANCE ACCOUNTS

Dynamics of

Traffic Court Interactions

RONALD V. COLEMAN

TRAFFIC COURTS ARE SITUATIONS of grievance
expression and social control of such expression. To appear in
traffic court rather than mail in one's fine is typically to feel
that the charge or the fine is unjust or otherwise imposes a
burden that requires countering. On the other side, the court
desires to define, manage, and process these grievances with
maximum order and minimum difficulty.

This report examines the encounter of these two potentially
and actually conflicting parties and scrutinizes three salient
aspects: the physical setting of its occurrence and the corre-
sponding social meaning of that setting; the process, structure
and dominance features of the encounter itself; and the play of
defendant's "accounts" and the judge's response to them. Each
is discussed in sequence.

AUTHOR'S NOTE: I am grateful to John Lofland for guidance, assistance,
and support.

[61]

The empirical materials related are drawn from four months' observation of the traffic court of a small, West Coast city. Exhaustive notes were made during and after court sessions and analyzed following the general guidelines of the "grounded theory" perspective (Glaser and Strauss, 1967; Lofland, 1974, forthcoming). The generalizations offered and conclusions stated are to be considered suggestive rather than definitive.

SUBORDINATION OF DEFENDANTS

The courtroom observed was divided into two zones by a three and one-half foot high wooden wall with two swinging doors for exiting and entering. In the defendants' zone there were ten rows of twenty seats beginning two feet in back of the dividing wall and running all the way back against the opposite wall. A hat and coat rack, beige painted walls, and three 10′ x 12′ picture glass windows with venetian blinds (which were always closed) were situated behind the defendants and facing the judge. Defendants, witnesses, lawyers, and observers waited in this area. The judge's zone contained a clock and thermostat (which was adjacent to a green "exit" sign above a yellow, reinforced steel door directly behind the judge's podium), a clerk's desk, a small step-stairs leading to the judge's podium which was 12′ x 3′ and included a desk made of solid oak, a tall, thickly foam-padded revolving chair, a witness box next to the podium, a lawyer's desk surrounded by eight foam-padded reinforced steel seats, the state and national flags situated a foot from the wall behind the judge's podium, a large, green chalk board placed in front of the witness box, and a jury box. The judge, clerk, and a defendant (at times there were several defendants in the judge's zone waiting for receipts or other documents from the clerk) constituted the personnel.

This physical setting manifested some important social contrasts. (1) Rows of chairs in the defendants' zone were linked together by two board planks lying underneath the chairs so that when defendants moved in their chairs, other chairs in the row also moved. This "bond" symbolized the defendants' common linkage, or the "common fate" awaiting them in the ensuing encounter. (2) The defendants' zone was characterized by small chairs, bare walls, dull colors, absence of decorative objects and windows which were covered; that is, "aesthetic deprivation." The judge's area included large, foam-padded, steel-reinforced oak chairs, a variety of colorful artifacts and objects—flags, a clock, and chalkboards—which gave the zone an aesthetic quality relative to the defendants' area. (3) The object arrangement of the defendants' zone tended to "violate normal spatial relationships." For example, the seats were so small and close together that when defendants were summoned they often had difficulty walking down the aisle without bumping into knees and stepping on toes.

ENCOUNTER PROCESS, STRUCTURE, AND FUNCTION

In this physical subordination of common fate, aesthetic deprivation, and spatial violation, the actual encounters played through three main phases.

Preencounter Pomp

Grievers gathered in the courtroom from 8:30 to 8:55 A.M. for the court opening of 9:00 A.M. However, the court always started about ten minutes late. Defendants sat or stood and waited. At times, there was quiet chattering. The hum of the ventilation system was usually quite noticeable. The waiting period amplified the suspense and anxiety among defendants— "I wonder what the judge is like?"—"I hope my case goes well." The defendants were, in a sense, special deviants. They had not only been labeled deviants—"You are accused of violation of . . ."—but had rejected that label by their very presence. Almost all were there to lodge a grievance. The message from the court to such grievers was that the "stigmatized" should be made to wait; thus, the seemingly harmless wait subtly degraded the defendants.

The waiting period ended with the entrance of the judge, a conservatively groomed man wearing a dark suit and tie (no robe) and short hair which was greased and combed closely to his head. He carried many folders (defendants' files) under his right arm and was followed closely by the clerk, a middle-aged woman in a dress who was also carrying files. The judge ascended the small step-stairs. Putting the files down and sitting in the chair, all of his body was hidden except his shoulders and head. In this position, his upper body towered over defendants standing before him. This pomp and positioning seemed to function to surround the judge with an aura of almost holy reverence and respect; and defendants should behave accordingly.

Arraignment Statement

Immediately after sitting, the judge launched into a pre-encounter arraignment statement:

> Court will be in order. Has everyone checked with the clerk in the front? Are there any lawyers representing clients? Ladies and Gentlemen, I am here to advise you that you are entitled to the services of an attorney and that if you cannot afford one the court will appoint one. You're entitled to a public and speedy trial which in these cases means within 45 days of today's date. You have a right to have it dismissed if it is not tried within 45 days. You may confront witnesses, subpoena others, and testify on your own behalf. In most of these cases you may enter a plea of not guilty and request a trial. You may enter a plea of nolo contendere; that is, you do not admit the charges but you do not wish to contest the charges. This has the same effect of a plea of guilty on your record but cannot normally be used against you in any other proceedings. You are allowed, in most of these cases, a reasonable continuance. And finally, you can plead guilty and have me dispose of it this morning. Are there any questions? [a pause of two to three seconds] If not, I would ask that you come forward and step behind the desk when your name is called.

The arraignment statement was given only at this point and was thus a mass apprising of rights and responsibilities.

Defendants never subsequently asked questions about their rights even though an enormous amount of information had been quickly conveyed. Many seemed not to have understood or listened to the statement. When they approached the bench the judge often had to selectively reiterate some of their rights and responsibilities. In addition, the statement presaged the bureaucratic character of the encounter between judge and defendants. The encounter had two objectives: a plea by the defendants and a final disposition by the judge. The statement was implicitly a declaration and outline of how the encounter should ideally proceed and also functioned to communicate the rules of the encounter, which were defined in rigid, bureaucratic terms.

Interchange

With little variation, the judge-griever encounter had seven phases. (1) In the "calling-forth" phase the defendant's name was announced and he was given a "brief-greet" ("Good morning!" or "How are you?"). (2) The "accusation" phase presented the charge (e.g., "The problem this morning is alleged speed.") and requested a plea ("What's your pleasure?"), with only slight variations. (3) The defendants entered a "plea": (a) not guilty; (b) guilty, including guilty with proof of correction as in showing proof of correcting faulty tail lights and guilty with a not guilty stipend as in disclaiming responsibility for an admitted offense (e.g., "Yes the motorcycle was illegally parked but somebody had moved it out of the legal designated parking place to an illegal one!"); (c) nolo contendere; and, (d) no entrance of a plea, including by-passing the entrance of a plea by going directly into an account or requesting a continuance. Infrequently there were vacillating pleas: grievers kept changing their minds from guilty to not guilty and ended by either asking for time to "think it over" or requesting a continuance. (4) "Accounts" followed pleas, expressed the grievances of defendants, and were either requested by the judge, or entered without much prompting, as in this encounter:

J [Judge] : The problem is alleged speed. What's your pleasure?

D [Defendant] Ah, not guilty. Gee, yesterday I received this warrant notice.[1]

(5) In the "response" phase, the judge counter-argued, questioned, or lectured on the alleged complaint offered in the defendant's account:

D: Pardon me, but I'm new to the city. The intersection, are you familiar with it? [Judge nods] Oh, it is a tricky one.

J: However, there is a sign which warns of a stop sign. Whenever one is new to an area they should be extra careful. If you went through the stop sign, as you say you did, then I have no choice.

(6) The "resolution" phase began with defendants acknowledging a choice: "I'll take the fine"; "I'll talk to the police"; "I think I'll continue this"; "I'll go to trial"; and so on. It continued with the judge acknowledging the choice, "I've entered your plea of not guilty"; asking further questions, "Do you have the money today to pay?"; or supplying further explanations, "This matter will be continued until December 4th." This phase ended with an explanation of official procedure, "You may post the bail with the clerk"; "You may pick up the receipt, post bail and receive a list of referrals from the clerk"; and so on. (7) The final phase, "conclusionary remarks," signaled propriety between the judge and defendants:

D: Hey, thank you your honor.

J: Surely.

D: Is that all your honor?

J: That's it!

D: Thanks.

J: Certainly.[2]

Structural Features

The physical setting and the social meaning of that setting and the three major phases of courtroom interaction—pre

encounter pomp, arraignment statement, encounter interchange—displayed six, salient structural features. (1) "Distance"
between judge and defendants was accentuated. During an
encounter the physical distance between the two was at least
fifteen feet, the podium (12' x 5') itself was a "fortress, deep
and mighty," conveying a sense of impenetrability. In addition,
the lawyer's desk, situated between the podium and the
defendant's "place," served as a barrier between defendants and
the judge. And, the clerk acted as an intermediary agent who
handed documents back and forth between the judge and
defendants. Thus, the judge "strove," functionally, to establish
distance, both socially and physically from defendants. (2) The
judge was seated above the standing defendants (the "revered"
character). He initiated nearly all questions and subtly degraded
and heightened suspense by allowing defendants to wait. It was
appropriately symbolic that the room thermostat was periodi-
cally adjusted on the judge's direction to the clerk. An
"atmosphere" communicating domination was thusly suggested.
(3) The courtroom process had a socialization effect on the
defendants. The effect of the process at each phase was to bring
about important changes in the defendants, such that they
learned to go through the process in a way which was most
efficient and least threatening to the court.[3] These changes
were messages from those in control that functioned to define
the situation in their favor. At each phase of the process new
messages were communicated, transforming the existing definition of the situation into an emerging new definition. Each
phase was full of these transformations. Thus, the waiting and
entering phase functioned to make certain impressions on the
defendants, such as building suspense. These served to define
the existing situation as suspenseful. The calling-forth phase
began with the judge announcing the defendant's name so that
he would come forward. Here, the *felt transformation* was the
defendant's realization that he would be individually called
forth and separated from his peers (the new situation) who up
to this point in the process were being treated as a group (the
old situation). What started out as mass group justice ended

with groupless and unsupported individuals disengaged from a common environment. The transformation of situations was remarkably quick and seemed rather traumatic for defendants.[4] (4) The preencounter arraignment statement defined the situation in rigid terms by outlining the steps of the encounter. The statement channeled and toned down grievance by ignoring accounts—the actual backbone of the encounter in the griever's eyes. Because of the potential disruptive nature of complaints, it gave order in a situation of potential disorder. Rigidity was also especially apparent in the initiation of all questions and guidance through the steps of the encounter by the judge. (5) The judge processed an enormous number of cases (thirty to forty) in an hour. He heard twenty to twenty-five thousand cases in one year. Rapidity was an organizational imperative. The arraignment statement, in its mass apprising of rights, situational precedents (allowing him to skip lecturing) and the standard format of the encounter (accusation, plea, account, and so on) all facilitated the *rapidity* of justice. (6) The judge was able to operate effectively because the courtroom process was largely prescribed (plea, account, and so on). This standard format or prescript facilitated *routinization.*

Defendant's grievances were potentially disruptive to the legitimacy and integrity of the court and to the social order in general. The maintenance of social distance, the domination of the interaction by the judge, the socialization of defendants to the delegated role of "defendant," and proceeding through the process in a specific fashion (routine), with certain boundaries (rigidity) and in a quick fashion (rapidity), functioned, however, to define and *control* the situation in the court's favor.

Accounts and the judge's responses to them were the heart of the encounter. Defendants had an opportunity to lodge grievances and the judge, as a target, had to manage them.

GRIEVANCE ACCOUNTS

Nearly all defendants who came before the judge expressed some sort of discontent or pain—grief, regarding their citation—

and sought some sort of compensation, such as dismissal, a reduction in the fine, a referral, a continuance, or a trial. Regardless of the plea grievers entered, they were expressing discontent with existing conditions and solicited compensation. Following Scott and Lyman (1968: 47) it was important to distinguish between accounts that were excuses and those that were justifications.[5]

Excuses

An excuse was the denial of responsibility and went as far as to deny the act occurred. Four tactical excuses were utilized by grievers. (1) In resorting to "official documents" and "technical verifications," such items as pictures and speedometer checks with an official certification were effective in verifying innocence or casting doubt on the validity of the citation:

> D: I wasn't going sixty-five like the ticket says. My speedometer is off. I had it tested. Here is the notice of official clock by the C.H.P. which shows the cable off.
>
> J: May I see that? Bring that forward. [defendant gives verification to judge] Yes, very well, case is dismissed.

(2) Grievers resorted to "logical proofs":

> J: What's your pleasure?
>
> D: Not guilty. I couldn't have gone thirty-five because I never got out of first gear. See, I just turned out of the driveway and pulled up to a stop sign which is about twenty feet from where I live. I never had the chance to go that fast, let along going thirty-five in first gear in a Volkswagen.

(3) In "nonoccurrence," grievers overtly denied responsibility for the act: "there was no way I was going seventy, sixty yes, but not seventy"; "as far as I could see there is no parking sign." Or they denied the act even occurred: "I was absolutely not tail-gating"; "I didn't have my lights off, let alone speeding"; and, "I wasn't driving so how could I be charged

with it." (4) "Deferred responsibility" displaced culpability elsewhere (usually onto some other person), as in: "I sold my car a month ago so I figured it [a citation given the defendant] was his [the new owner] problem"; "It's really up to the university to supply adequate parking facilities"; "I have to park somewhere"; "It wasn't my fault, but my brother's it was [sic]"; "I had to speed up to change lanes because of this other guy who was lagging"; "I left someone watching the car, the police told me it's ok to park there if someone is watching it."

Through the utilization of excuse tactics grievers hoped to gain compensation by managing and defining the overall texture and content of the account as sensible, rational, credible, and logical. This was accomplished by relying on "socially legitimate" forms of accountability—official documents, technical verifications, logical proofs, denying the act occurred, and deferred responsibility. Thus, the function of excuses was to convey the impression that the account was plausible.

Justifications

Justifications were ambiguous in that defendants accepted responsibility (pleaded guilty) but asserted there were more important elements which if taken into consideration warranted a compensation. There were seven main justification tactics utilized by grievers.

(1) "Externalities beyond control" must be considered when rendering justice: "I was in jail"; "my children are having problems"; "I haven't fixed it because it broke down two weeks ago . . . it's off the road"; "The day after I got the ticket my car was wrecked. I really haven't had the chance to take care of it." (2) Grievers acknowledged responsibility but asserted a higher moral rule (a "higher involvement") was more important at the time of the violation: "I was upset because of a threat to my sister, I forgot"; "My children were horsing, screaming, you know, I thought something was wrong. I didn't see the light"; "My little girl was terribly sick, so sick, I was rushing her to the hospital"; "I had been studying, thinking about other things."

(3) In the "appeal to common humanity" tactic, grievers attempted to strike a chord of sympathy with the judge by referring to common human mistakes, predicaments, and problems: "I haven't had a ticket in twelve years"; "I don't like to park far away at night because of the distance to the library"; "I don't have any money . . . I'm trying to get a job and I'm in the middle of moving the family up"; "I've been working on the car for a couple of months . . . It was the first time I've had it on the road. All I did was to drive up the block and look what happened." (4) The "honest-direct" or "confessional approach" functioned as a reverse tactic, was rare, and usually effective in gaining compensation. While many grievers recited and constructed long and elaborate explanations, honest-direct or confessional grievers flattered the judge. It was almost as if defendants were saying: "Ok, you caught me, I confess"; or "Here are the bare facts, let them speak for themselves." For example, "I was speeding to show off"; "I was testing my new wheels out"; "I blew it"; "I'd like it reduced."[6] (5) Occasionally, grievers would "point out trivial irrelevancies" when other tactics were unavailable or had been expended. For example, "The cop was confused. Look-it-here, he spelled my name wrong, my address, too." In attempting to conform to the ritualistic steps by utilizing such a tactic there was a risk the judge would find such "irrelevancies," annoying and distracting. Thus, this tactic often brought about the wrath of the judge. (6) In the "greater-than-or-equal-to" account grievers accepted responsibility but pointed out that others committed equal or greater crimes: "I was going with traffic"; "I counted, on another occasion, 157 cars which passed me in a half-hour and I was only going the same as I was when I was given a ticket"; "the officer ran into me, I had to go to the hospital, then they greet me with a ticket afterwards. I just don't think it is fair to fine me." (7) Lastly, highly manipulative and astute defendants often utilized the "any account" tactic. The defendants pleaded guilty and then recited most any explanation, however absurd or questionable: "I'm guilty, but I'm not. I just wasn't myself that day"; "I'm guilty but not totally . . . my girl friend was helping me drive . . . I was 'clutchin-it', she had the stick."[7]

Justifications functioned to manage plausibility and, in addition, served to gain sympathy, provide for an empathic identification between judge and defendants, appeal to what was basically a white, middle-class sense of ethics, and affirm the ritualistic phases of the encounter itself. First, justification tactics such as externalities beyond control and the appeal to common humanity attempted to gain sympathetic understanding from the judge. In the latter tactic, for example, a woman complained that parking a long distance from her destination raised her fear of an assault. She attempted to solicit the judge's sympathy by appealing to his protectiveness of women. Second, defendants often hoped to strike an empathic identification with the judge. For example, a defendant utilizing the greater-than-or-equal-to tactic explained that the day after he received a ticket his car was wrecked. Hence, he had not had a chance to move the car and fix the broken tail-light. Third, higher involvement strove to appeal to what was basically a white, middle-class sense of ethics. For example, a defendant explained that he had been studying diligently for his school finals so he was not able to be as attentive as usual while driving. Last, the trivial irrelevancies, honest confessional and any account tactics functioned to affirm the ritualistic and routinized phases of the encounter.[8]

COOLING THE GRIEVER OUT

Grievances had to be managed so as to communicate a sense that justice prevailed. As a target for grievance, the judge had developed such effective strategies of handling grievances. The judge's response to defendants exemplified the generic situation of grievance management, the difficult task of cooling the griever out (Goffman, 1952; Blumberg, 1967: 67-69).

Cooling the griever out entailed getting defendants to accept the conditions of the final disposition, conditions that were nearly always dissonant with their goals. This involved managing defendants such that despite not receiving the desired compensation they at least felt that justice prevailed. There were two main forms of cooling the griever out: disposition bargaining and adhering to the bureaucratic ideal, including in the latter, a resort to legalistic rules and the appeal to the abstruse.

Disposition Bargaining

Disposition bargaining was a form of plea bargaining where the judge offered a resolution to the problem if defendants would accept partial compensation. There were three tactics of dispositioning bargaining. (1) In "scouts honor" the judge requested a promise from defendants (which could not be legally sanctioned) in exchange for a partial compensation: "If you promise me the car won't touch the street until this is corrected, I'll dismiss the charge"; "I'll reduce the charge on the condition you'll write the traffic committee." (2) When case processing was behind schedule the judge skipped a lengthy response to accounts given by defendants. Thus, he utilized the "take-into-consideration" tactic: "I understand your problem. I'll take that into consideration and reduce the fine to $10.00"; "I'm willing to take your account into consideration and reduce the fine to $20.00." (3) In "scolding" the judge reminded defendants of their responsibilities with a slap-on-the-wrist: "I'll dismiss the charge of failure to appear with the warning that a ticket is in place of being arrested on the spot. When you fail to appear, it is dead time for you, me, and the police." Or in cases where defendants were charged with two or more crimes the judge would discard one case, with a warning, then hold defendants completely liable for the other.

The tactics of disposition bargaining enabled the court to maintain the impression that it considered all grievances worthy, while it effectively filtered-out the case load and maintained court integrity. Scouts honor cooled-out grievers by flattering them. "If you promise" implied the judge trusted them (which was flattering) when indeed he was likely relieved to be rid of such trivial cases. Grievers departed without the compensation desired, but at least felt the judge respected

them. The take-into-consideration tactic functioned to cool
grievers because the judge ignored or pretended he believed the
obviously absurd account. Here again, grievers left with the
feeling of having outwitted the organization when in fact they
had been effectively managed. Scolding served to communicate
to defendants that they were fortunate since they could receive
harsher sanctions. This functioned to neutralize the grievance
by playing a type of one-upmanship ("you owe me one").
Disposition bargaining cooled grievers by changing the focus,
flattering and neutralizing the grievances, and leaving defendants with the feeling they had outwitted the organization. Such
tactics protected the court from having to come to terms with
questionable or absurd accounts, or with the grievance itself. In
this sense, the integrity of the court was maintained.

Adhering to the Bureaucratic Ideal

Disposition bargaining was not utilized in serious cases such
as drunk driving. Informal activities were even omitted from the
encounter process as in the judge asking "How are you?" or
"Good morning!" The judge became quite formal and relied on
a bureaucratic ideal (the preencounter arraignment statement)
to guide him through the process:

J: Mr. Vincent [fictitious name] The charge is violation of vehicle
code 444444; driving while under the influence of intoxicating
liquors. What is your plea?

D: Not guilty.

J: Do you have an attorney?

D: No, I'm unemployed.

J: I shall appoint you one. Which day do you want for trial,
December 4th or 28th?

D: December 4th.

J: Alright. I have written the name of the attorney you may contact
and have set bail at $125. Are there any questions?

D: Nope.

In such cases, accounts were rarely submitted or requested. This strict adherence to the bureaucratic model functioned to maintain the definition throughout the encounter that the situation was serious.

The judge also used the bureaucratic ideal to cool-off grievances which were viewed as special threats. (1) "Resort to legalistic rules" was utilized in situations of threat in both mild and serious cases. It functioned to cool-off the most vehement of grievers. The theme was that legal rules transcend (were the highest entity) accounts:

> D: Look, I had been studying; thinking about other things. Besides there wasn't any cars coming.
>
> J: Mr. Vincent, as long as there is a stop sign instead of a yield sign, I have to stop, you have to stop, the police have to stop.
>
> D: I sold the car a month ago so I figured it was his problem.
>
> J: The citation was issued while you were still the legal owner. You are responsible, under the law, for any citation while you are still the legal owner.

(2) By "resort to the abstruse" the judge responded to the complaints by referring to abstruse and sacred ideals:

> D: I don't like to park far away because of the distance . . . It's dark and really far. There are no parking places closer.
>
> J: I can't really deal with that here. It's a policy decision to be made elsewhere.
>
> D: I'd really like for you to dismiss this.
>
> J: I won't do that. Only if it is shown to be illegal or unconstitutional can I strike it down.

Utilized in situations of threat, these latter tactics functioned to cool-off the grievers. The judge's responses were vague, unobtainable in concrete terms, and therefore resistant to further questioning or probes. Such statements as: "illegal and unconstitutional"; "policy decision to be made elsewhere"; "I have to stop, you have to stop, the police have to stop"; and, "you are responsible, under the law" were intimidating, irrelevant to the immediate needs of the grievers, and functioned to terminate further discussion along the lines of the complaints.

Nonetheless, these tactics conveyed the impression that the grievance account had been carefully considered. The tactics of cooling-the-mark-out functioned to manage the encounter and maintained that a sense of justice prevailed.

INITIATIVE AND COMPLIANCE

Accounts were not mentioned in the formal, preencounter arraignment statement of the court. That is, there was no formal recognition that during the encounter defendants would lodge grievances. Accounts were, in a sense, deviations from the formal system which had become institutionalized. They were what Selznick (1948: 27) terms the "unwritten laws." The organizational act of delegation "involves concrete individuals who have interests and goals which do not always coincide with the goals of the organization" (Selznick, 1948: 27). A central goal of the court was to control the threat of grievance by processing cases rapidly and efficiently. The goal of defendants was the redress of grievance or at least a sense that justice prevailed. Furthermore, "individual personalities may offer resistance to the demands made upon them" by the court (Selznick, 1948: 27).

Many grievers interpreted the opportunity to give an account in such a fashion that the interpretation of the role of "griever" was in contradiction to the court delegated and institutionalized role. The most common individual deviations were lengthy, or overextended accounts, which because of the demand for the rapidity of justice, profundly irritated the judge.[9] Hence, in the situation of overextension of grievance accounts the judge utilized several dramaturgical tactics (Goffman, 1959: 240-242). (1) "Somatic intimidation" involved the judge leaning forward with his forearms resting on his desk, his shoulders hunched forward, head extended outward in a ostrich-like fashion and staring, usually with a frown, at the defendants. (2) The judge expressed his "existential detachment" from the plight of grievers by yawning, staring off in the distance, leaning back in his chair with his hands grasped together behind his head, removing his glasses, passing his hand over his face, and rubbing his eyes. (3) Moreover, there was a general "somatic hyperactivity," or increase in body movement by the judge, including: heavy sighing, rocking back and forth in his chair, looking to and fro, and waving his arms and hands.

These nonverbal, subtle tactics were indicators to grievers that their accounts were taking too much time. When these tactics failed to pressure grievers into discontinuing, the judge utilized stronger and more overt tactics. (1) The judge issued "verbal cautions" as a warning to grievers not to consume too much time. Two of the judge's favorites were: "Because, because?" and "Briefly, briefly!":

> J: What's your pleasure?
> D: Not guilty.
> J: Because, because?

> J: What's your pleasure?
> D: Not guilty, and I'd like to tell why.
> J: Briefly, briefly!

(2) By means of indirect "verbal sanctions" the judge will quicken the process along with strong and intimidating language. The most frequently used were: "What brings you to me?" and "What do you want to do? What do you want to do?"

Grievers sometimes seemed intimidated, overwhelmed, and frustrated by the efficient court process, its impersonalization, and oppression. In order to deal with this opposite difficulty the judge appeared to utilize tactics of facilitating comfort including such devices as: (1) the "brief-greet," as in the cheery comments "Good morning!" and "How are you?"; (2) the "kind accusation"—"The problem this morning is alleged speed. What's your pleasure?"; (3) "kind intermediary remarks," such as "take your time"; "Sit down, think it over, and let me know when you are ready"; (4) "kind conclusionary remarks," such as "You bet"; "Surely"; and, "at your leisure"; (5) "situational precedents"—grievers were forsaken lectures by being referred to an example of a similiar, previous case; and, (6) "mass apprising of rights" allowing grievers time to contemplate and prepare for their accounts.

Defendants' accounts, a time limit on those accounts, and the judge's responses had become institutionalized. They were part of the "unwritten law", important for the effective functioning of the court which was an opportunity for individuals to express grievances and achieve a sense that justice prevailed, and to cool-out grievances. The problem arose that much of the controlled, efficient court process—both the formal and institutionalized informal systems—could be too impersonal and thus oppressive to the defendant's initiative ("individual interests and goals," Selznick, 1948: 27). That is, for defendants to feel that justice prevailed there had to be some "slippage" between the formally delegated role and the individual personality. A sense of justice was derived from this "slippage," this social "crack." The judge utilized devices of facilitating comfort in order to encourage defendants' initiative and convey a sense of justice in an oppressive situation. The problem however, was that the individuals' initiative came into conflict with the demand for compliance. Grievers too often supplied lengthy accounts. Hence, the judge utilized dramaturgical tactics, both subtle and overt, to deal with overextended accounts. Thus, the dilemma was that the court gave the opportunity to defendants to redesign the role in an effort to get them to accept it. The court encouraged initiative (an account) while demanding compliance (a short account). The judge was nonetheless, and for the most part, effective in managing the dilemma. The use of the above tactics functioned to maximize initiative and compliance among defendants, therefore maintaining the defendants' commitment to the court process.

MANAGING INTRAROLE CONFLICT

The observed judge appeared to suffer intrarole conflict (c.f., Goode, 1961). His role demanded that he be personally involved and sympathetic to the grievers while it also expected stern and uncompromising commitment to the rules. He was supposed to be a humanitarian as well as a rule enforcer. These role demands often clashed because grievers insisted that the judge be a humanitarian at the expense of a rule enforcer. The judge utilized various tactics to deal with this situation of intrarole conflict. The main coping tactic was to assert priorities. Rule enforcement had priority over humanitarianism whenever there was a test of his loyalties.

> D: My little girl was very sick. I was rushing her to the hospital.
>
> J: The risks of high speeds are too great. You should have called the police or an ambulance.

When the conflict was intense the judge utilized the "dispersion" tactic, referring grievers to other organizations.

> D: It's outrageous that they issue more parking permits than there are spaces. In fact, they issued 4,000 permits and there are only 3,600 parking places available.
>
> J: I can only go by what the police request. This is a policy decision to be made elsewhere. I'd like for you, although I can't make you, to bring this to the attention of the traffic committee. I'll also recommend that you take this problem up with the city council.

By "resorting to the abstruse" the judge settled the conflict by calling upon vague and cherished abstractions.

> D: The policeman pulled two of us over at the same time. The other guy was going much faster and the officer even told me the other guy was going a lot faster than me. Then he gives me a ticket, and says "I better cite you too. I think you were speeding." I wasn't, your honor.
>
> J: Well, the problem is I can't speculate on what may or may not have happened. I can only throw it out if it is shown to me to be illegal or unconstitutional.

In "deferring responsibility" the judge held other organizations responsible for the defendant's precarious position: "I don't adopt the laws, your representatives do"; "I can't possibly make such a decision . . . It's beyond me and the function of this court"; "My hands are tied, but, I'll give you three alternatives: I'll reduce the fine to three dollars, you may plead not guilty or what I'd really like you to do, although I can't make you, is to report this to the traffic committee in the form of a letter or see Lt. Doe of the police department." The judge under-cut appeals to higher morality by leveling and asserting we are all equal-under-the-law: "As long as there is a stop sign instead of a yield sign, I have to stop, you do, and the police do. Until that's changed I have to go along with it." The judge resolved the pressing conflict by asserting that "we all suffer." He pointed to the rules which impose on everyone: "The parking situation is bad. It's an irritation to you and to me."

The "assertion of priorities" indicated the judge's obligation. His sympathy may have been with grievers but his decisions and loyalties were to those various organized publics (e.g., the police and the community traffic committee) which possessed the most power. When the pressure mounted from powerful groups, the judge did not hesitate to "assert priority" in a blatant fashion.[10] Although this was an effective strategy, the judge seemed to prefer not to use it since he was an elected official who was attempting to maintain the loyalty of his constituents, many of whom were defendants. Thus, the "assert priority" tactic accented the dilemma of loyalty. It was strategically wiser to utilize other tactics. "Dispersion" and "deferring responsibility" functioned to include other organizations as responsible entities even though those organizations were not immediately available for use, and to spread and buffer the conflict.[11] "Resorting to the abstruse" confused the issue by bringing in sacred language and assumptions. The judge directed the definition of the situation from the pragmatic to the abstract. These abstractions could not be immediately contested. Lastly, "leveling" and "we all suffer" attempted to convince grievers of a common predicament. Thus, with the exception of "asserting priorities" the judge did not overtly indicate whether he sided with defendants or various powerful publics. The tactics of managing intrarole conflict were indirect and, therefore, diluted the immediate demands of competing publics. Nonetheless, the consequences of buffering and spreading the conflict, removing the definition of the situation from the pragmatic to the abstract and pointing to a common predicament resulted in the judge siding with the demands of the powerful groups.

SUBSTANCE AND EFFECTIVENESS: A SUMMARY AND IRONY

The physical setting of the courtroom subordinated defendants by altering their normal relationship to the social environment. Courtroom interaction was characterized by distancing, a socialization process which subjugated defendants, rigidity, rapidity and a routinized bureaucratic structure. The overriding function was to control the situation in order that the inherent threat of grievance would be contained. Grievance strategies utilized by defendants included excuses, which attempted to convince the judge that the grievance was plausible, and justifications which attempted to solicit and appeal to the judge's moral sensibilities. Defendants had to be careful not to offend court integrity with their accounts and thus incur the wrath of the judge while at the same time stretching their accounts in order to gain as much compensation as possible. In cooling-out the grievers, the judge had effectively to manage grievances by convincing defendants that justice had prevailed while maintaining court integrity in situations of threat. In situations of over-extended girevances the judge utilized dramaturgical strategies to terminate such deviations. In considering that grievance accounts allowed for individual initiative in what was otherwise an impersonalized and oppressive situation, the judge, nonetheless, had to utilize strategies of facilitating comfort in order to allow for initiative and personalize the encounter.[12] Lastly, the judge's management of intrarole conflict temporarily alleviated the demands for loyalties from competing publics. Most of the tactics made vague the immediate commitment of the judge, yet the consequences of such indirectness was to favor powerful, organized groups.

The traffic arraignment court reported on here was flexible and effective in filtering-out grievances. However, the court lacked true substance. It was potentially vulnerable and weak. All grievers had to do to obtain full hearing of a grievance was to plead not guilty and demand a trial. As an arraignment court, such a request had to be legally granted. Most grievers compromised and bargained for some variety of compensation, usually economic. It is in this sense that the traffic arraignment court was weak and lacked substance but yet effective in the management of grievances.

NOTES

1. Accounts, and the responses to them, were occasionally skipped in continuous cases (ones which had been delayed or deferred), when there had been a request for a continuance and when defendants pleaded nolo contendere. In such cases the final disposition phase followed the plea phase.

2. Two major contingencies played upon and modified this typical encounter process. First, in serious cases (i.e., drunk driving as opposed to illegal parking, faulty equipment and the like), it was more likely the judge adhered to the bureaucratic character as outlined in the arraignment statement (discussed in "adhering to the bureaucratic ideal"). Second, in the course of a morning the judge would come across several cases of the same variety. In order to avoid restatements he asked defendants if they had heard the prior lecture on the same case situation. If defendants acknowledged that they had, both the account and response phase were bypassed and the case was quickly resolved.

3. As Blumberg notes, the court "socializes its members and participants toward compliance with specific objectives which are not part of the official goals of justice and due process." Specific objectives are court efficiency, production, and the disposal of the maximum number of cases (Blumberg, 1967: 70, 119, 170).

4. Interviews with acquaintances and my own several appearances in this court, at least, suggested a situationally traumatic character to the experience.

5. The concepts of excuse and justification are drawn from Scott and Lyman (1968). However, the terms are defined differently in this report.

6. This last variation, however, ran the risk of disrupting the ritual. It was not wise to be overly candid as in "I'd like this dismissed." This threatened to disregard the ritualistic steps by ignoring or skipping over the account phase. The judge seemed

not to like to skip phases, perhaps because that posed a threat, a revelation of what the court was predominantly doing: pretending to take mild cases seriously, which in fact were hardly worth the court's time and effort. (Seemingly, the judge would welcome the skipping of phases in favor of greater efficiency and rapidity of justice. However, it is my argument that such ritualistic phases maintained the impression that the "due process of law" was being upheld.) Hence, there was an inherent dilemma in this tactic. On the one hand, grievers gained compensation through candidness. On the other hand, such candid behavior often ran the risk of disrupting the ritualistic and routinized court process and therefore incurring the loss of compensation.

7. Accounts which were too absurd, nonsensical or irrational posed the threat of disrupting the integrity of the court. One organizational demand was for efficiency and rapidity of justice. If the judge rejected too many absurd accounts, grievers would likely demand trials and the case load would become burdensome. On the other hand, the problem for grievers was to manage accounts such that they seemed genuine. The judge had to be convinced of the genuineness of the grievances and the grievers. Paradoxically, the account could not just be "any account" but rather had to be genuine, which of course was problematic and susceptible to the degree that the court was burdened with cases.

8. The functions of grievance accounts were, however, diverse and overlapping.

9. See also Mileski, 1971: 516, who has noted the defendant who "talks too much."

10. Judges who "assert priority" in favor of defendants may become embedded in controversy with powerful publics. See, for example, Gibson, 1975: A1 and A8.

11. Blumberg notes that Metropolitan judges diffuse responsibility and authority in order to alleviate formal obligations: "Reluctant to shoulder the decision-making burden . . . there are ample intermediaries and groups who can be invoked to share in the responsibilities which are ultimately those of the judge" (Blumberg, 1967: 180).

12. Another way of conceptualizing this dilemma, and leading to a further irony, is Blumberg's declaration of two models of criminal justice: the constitutional-ideological system of due process and the administrative, rational-bureaucratic system currently utilized (Blumberg, 1967: 169): "There is an almost irreconcilable conflict: intense pressure to process large numbers of cases . . . and the . . . ideological and legal requirements of 'due process of law'." The dilemma is resolved or managed "through bureaucratically ordained short cuts, deviations and outright rule violations by members of the court" (Blumberg, 1967: xi). In this study, overextended grievances violate "intense pressure to process," hence the judge utilized "short cuts," such as dramaturgical strategies. On the other hand, an oppressive and impersonalized rational-bureaucratic system, as in this court, violated ideological commitments to "due process of law." Thus, ironically, the judge utilized bureaucratic "short cuts" to facilitate comfort and therefore reassert commitments to the "due process of law."

not to like to skip phases, perhaps because that posed a threat, a revelation of what the court was predominantly doing: pretending to take mild cases seriously, which in fact were hardly worth the court's time and effort. (Seemingly, the judge would welcome the skipping of phases in favor of greater efficiency and rapidity of justice. However, it is my argument that such ritualistic phases maintained the impression that the "due process of law" was being upheld.) Hence, there was an inherent dilemma in this tactic. On the one hand, grievers gained compensation through candidness. On the other hand, such candid behavior often ran the risk of disrupting the ritualistic and routinized court process and therefore incurring the loss of compensation.

7. Accounts which were too absurd, nonsensical or irrational posed the threat of disrupting the integrity of the court. One organizational demand was for efficiency and rapidity of justice. If the judge rejected too many absurd accounts, grievers would likely demand trials and the case load would become burdensome. On the other hand, the problem for grievers was to manage accounts such that they seemed genuine. The judge had to be convinced of the genuineness of the grievances and the grievers. Paradoxically, the account could not just be "any account" but rather had to be genuine, which of course was problematic and susceptible to the degree that the court was burdened with cases.

8. The functions of grievance accounts were, however, diverse and overlapping.

9. See also Mileski, 1971: 516, who has noted the defendant who "talks too much."

10. Judges who "assert priority" in favor of defendants may become embedded in controversy with powerful publics. See, for example, Gibson, 1975: A1 and A8.

11. Blumberg notes that Metropolitan judges diffuse responsibility and authority in order to alleviate formal obligations: "Reluctant to shoulder the decision-making burden . . . there are ample intermediaries and groups who can be invoked to share in the responsibilities which are ultimately those of the judge" (Blumberg, 1967: 180).

12. Another way of conceptualizing this dilemma, and leading to a further irony, is Blumberg's declaration of two models of criminal justice: the constitutional-ideological system of due process and the administrative, rational-bureaucratic system currently utilized (Blumberg, 1967: 169): "There is an almost irreconcilable conflict: intense pressure to process large numbers of cases . . . and the . . . ideological and legal requirements of 'due process of law'." The dilemma is resolved or managed "through bureaucratically ordained short cuts, deviations and outright rule violations by members of the court" (Blumberg, 1967: xi). In this study, overextended grievances violate "intense pressure to process," hence the judge utilized "short cuts," such as dramaturgical strategies. On the other hand, an oppressive and impersonalized rational-bureaucratic system, as in this court, violated ideological commitments to "due process of law." Thus, ironically, the judge utilized bureaucratic "short cuts" to facilitate comfort and therefore reassert commitments to the "due process of law."

ODIS E. BIGUS is a doctoral student in sociology at the University of
California, San Francisco. His interests include research in the areas of
suburbanization, middle-class life styles, and alcoholism.

THE MILKMAN AND HIS CUSTOMER: *A Cultivated*

Relationship

ODIS E. BIGUS

AMERICA IS A SERVICE SOCIETY—so much so that
essentially nonservice institutions, such as stores, take on
service-like characteristics (Goffman, 1961: 326).[1] This em-
phasis on service has given rise to a preponderance of a
particular kind of social activity, which I will refer to as
"cultivating," and an associated kind of social relationship,
which I will refer to as a "cultivated relationship." "Cultivating" as it is used here refers to the courting and wooing
activities engaged in by servicers in relations with those whom
they service. Cultivating techniques are employed with the
intent of either directly or indirectly gaining a reward (usually
monetary). "Cultivated relationships" are relationships which

AUTHOR'S NOTE: I wish to express my thanks to Barney Glaser, Robert
Nicholson, Virginia Olesen, and Leonard Schatzman for their valuable
comments and suggestions on earlier drafts of this paper, and to E. Linwood
Tipton of the Milk Industry Foundation for providing me with information
about the retail milk business.

are carried out with the primary intent of gaining such a reward. They include but are not limited to service relationships. They are usually asymmetrical, with the less powerful[2] party utilizing cultivating tactics to bring the relationship closer to a state of symmetry.[3]

One such relationship—that between milkmen and their customers—will be discussed in this paper. The structure of the milkman-customer relationship, for reasons to be discussed below, is one of extreme asymmetry, with the milkman initially excercising very little control. However, by employing cultivating techniques, milkmen are able to transform this initially asymmetrical relationship into one which more closely approximates symmetry.

The information upon which the following discussion is based was obtained by my having been a milkman, in the San Francisco Bay Area, for a period of approximately fourteen months—from October 1965 to January 1967. The information derived from this was supplemented by subsequent informal interviews with my former co-workers, conducted mostly during the winter of 1968 and spring of 1969, with several interviews since that time.

My employment as a milkman was prior to my introduction to sociology, so that my own experiences were those of a "sociologically naive" social actor. Thus, I was one of my main informants. There is no reason, however, to believe that my experiences as a milkman were unique. Milkmen frequently share their experiences with one another, and mine were essentially the same as those reported by my co-workers; interviewing confirmed this. The anecdotes which I use for illustration are primarily from my own experiences; the instances were carefully chosen to represent typical experiences. I relate only occurrences similar to those commonly reported by my former co-workers.

The home delivery milk business is not a particularly homogeneous enterprise. Individual factors (population density, physical terrain, and so forth) in particular locations greatly affect the manner in which it is carried out. This makes general statements about milkmen difficult. Due to the fact that my observations were made in a single location with its own peculiarities, only some of what I say will apply generally. However, whether or not my discussion reflects other locations is not particularly important, as it is not my intent to give a general description of what milkmen do. I am interested in analyzing the process of cultivating. My interest in milkmen stems primarily from the fact that their activities mirror this process.

I will begin my discussion with an examination of the conditions which engender a need for milkmen to cultivate relationships. I will discuss both those conditions which are industry-wide and those which were present in the particular location I studied. I will follow this with a discussion of the particular cultivating techniques employed by the milkmen in this location. I will close with a short discussion of cultivating in general, as it relates to service relationships.

GENERATIVE CONDITIONS

Although it is rather difficult to make generalized statements about the home delivery milk business, it is evident that several cultural and technological changes have occurred over the past several decades which have affected it as a whole. Over this period, the retail sale of milk has gradually shifted from the milk truck to the grocery store. In the 1920s, almost all the milk consumed by American families was home delivered. Today only about fifteen to eighteen percent is home delivered, and this percentage is continuing to decline.[4] In response to this decline, retail distributors in many parts of the country have altered their operating procedures to such an extent that the milkman's job has been thoroughly changed. Under the conditions described below, it has been transformed from a job which at one time involved very little customer contact into a job in which active cultivation of customer relationships is an essential task. In the following section, I shall describe the structural conditions which have brought this change about. Following this, I shall describe the particular conditions present in the context of which I was a part, and which I subsequently studied.

Industry-Wide Factors

SUBURBANIZATION

A large factor in the decline of the home delivery milk business is suburbanization, which has produced "sprawling" areas with high population but relatively low density. It has become increasingly difficult for retail distributors to form routes which are economically profitable on the basis of sheer numbers of customers. To derive profit in this manner, a distributor must be able to form compact routes with low travel time between stops, which cannot be accomplished in areas characterized by low population density. The decrease in percentage of families receiving home delivery has an amplifying effect which makes this problem more severe. As fewer families receive home delivery, the space between customers becomes even greater, regardless of population density.

These two factors combined produce "spread out" routes whose potential for profit is low. As population density and the percentage of consumers receiving home delivery decreases, milk routes necessarily become smaller in terms of number of customers, but larger in terms of the distance traveled. Thus, modern milkmen generally have fewer customers, spaced farther apart, than did their predecessors.

However, even if a retail distributor were able to increase the number of his customers, economic profit would not necessarily result. Increasing the number of customers may decrease profit (Baumer et al., 1969). This apparent paradox is explained by the fact that a distributor can increase his potential for profit through acquiring more customers only if he can maintain a certain ratio regarding number of customers and volume of sales. If fifty low-consumption customers[5] are acquired by a distributor, his potential for profit would decrease, although his volume of sales would increase. The probability of new customers being high consumers is lessened by the fact that high-consumption customers tend already to receive home delivery, whereas low-consumption customers tend to purchase milk from grocery stores. However, this is changing as, proportionately, the number of high consumers terminating home delivery is greater than the number of low consumers doing so (Baumer et al., 1969: 3-5). This makes it increasingly difficult for retail distributors to maintain a satisfactory ratio between volume of sales and number of customers.

THE SUPERMARKET

The development of the modern supermarket is another factor which has contributed to the decline of the home delivery milk business. Most of the business lost by milkmen is inherited by supermarkets. However, it is not the presence of the supermarket per se which is responsible for milkmen losing their customers. Because of other cultural and technological changes, including the automobile, the refrigerator, and the decreased perishability of dairy products—and the increased availability of these items—the supermarket has become an accessible and convenient place from which to purchase milk and other dairy products (Baumer et al., 1969: 4). The modern housewife can drive to the local supermarket, purchase dairy products along with other groceries, return home, put these products in her refrigerator, and be assured that they will not sour for at least a week or so.

A CRITICAL PRICE DIFFERENTIAL

However, the increased availability and convenience of supermarkets does not necessarily assure the decline of the milkman. Although his services may no longer be necessary, they can be convenient, and thus remain desirable. The prime factor which reduces the desirability of home delivery (and increases the desirability of the supermarket) is price. Distribution through supermarkets is more economically efficient than distribution through home delivery—hence the retail price of milk distributed in this manner is lower—ordinarily by several cents per quart.

This price differential is an important factor in customers' decisions whether or not to purchase milk and other dairy products from a milkman.[6] According to a survey regarding consumer attitudes conducted in Cleveland and Columbus, Ohio, a large number (37%) of store customers would prefer home delivery if equal pricing existed (Baumer et al., 1969: 5). The percentage of high-consumption customers who would prefer home delivery if prices were equal is even greater (48%). And it is these customers who are most valuable to the milkman, as they reduce the ratio of number of customers to volume of sales and are therefore more potentially profitable.

DISTRIBUTOR COPING STRATEGIES

The foregoing factors have placed retail milk distributors in a rather tenuous position. In an effort to cope with this, they have made serveral adjustments in their operating procedures. Cumulatively, these adjustments have rather extensively changed the character of the home delivery business.

In general, the major problems with which distributors are faced are that their best customers are being siphoned off by supermarkets who have a crucial price advantage, and that their remaining customers are spread apart to such an extent that a milkman's ability to form profit-producing routes is greatly curtailed.

Very little can be done about the price disadvantage, as operating expenses are proportionately higher than those of the wholesale distributor.[7] In many areas, including the one in which I made my observations, the price differential between home delivery and the store is made manditory by law. Distributors in such areas must charge more whether they care to or not. In large part, then, retail distributors are unable to increase sales or attract new customers through a policy of price reduction. Furthermore, as I mentioned previously, profit does not necessarily result from an increase in number of customers anyway. To increase potential for profit, the ratio of number of customers to volume of sales must be reduced. In practical terms, the distributor must sell more, on the average, to each customer. In this manner, the relatively small size and diffuseness of the typical milk route can be at least partially compensated for.

Product diversification is a strategy which is often employed by retail distributors to achieve a greater rate of sales per customer. It is rather difficult to get customers to increase milk consumption, so to expand sales a larger variety of products must be offered. Thus, in areas in which the aforementioned conditions prevail, a large range of products is typically offered to home delivery customers. Within this range are a number of different kinds of dairy products (ice cream, cheese, yogurt, cottage cheese, and the like), as well as many nondairy products (such as flavored drinks, eggs, bacon, cosmetics, laundry soap). This wide range of products was not sold by milkmen when home delivery was the chief method of milk distribution.

Another strategy employed by retail distributors to cope with their increasingly unfavorable position has been to decrease the number of deliveries to each customer, which reduces operating costs and increases the number of customers to whom each milkman can deliver. Actually, this strategy was somewhat unintentional. During World War II, to conserve manpower, gasoline, and so forth, frequency of delivery was reduced to every other day or to three days per week. Most distributors continued these lower frequencies after the war because customers had become accustomed to them, and the economic advantage of less frequent delivery had been demonstrated (Roadhouse and Henderson, 1950: 501). The most common frequency of delivery today is three per week (Baumer et al., 1969: 9), although some distributors have recently experimented with less frequent delivery. Modern milkmen typically deliver to two sets of customers, each set receiving delivery three times per week. In effect, then, they conduct two routes, or as they put it, one route with two "sides."

Another procedure which has been changed by many distributors is the time of delivery. In the past, delivery was made very early in the morning so that customers would receive fresh milk before breakfast. Because of the present widespread use of refrigeration in the home, this is no longer necessary.[8] For those distributors who have resoted to product diversification, it is not only unnecessary, it is also inexpedient. These distributors find it advantageous to have their milkmen deliver during the day. At this time, personal contact with customers is much more likely than at early hours. Under these circumstances drivers are ordinarily required, or a least strongly encouraged, to seek out such contact and to employ appropriate tactics to increase sales.

A major impetus for the use of cultivating tactics, then, is the desire of distributors, brought about by their tenuous position, to increase their rate of sales per customer. By increasing their range of products, employing daytime delivery, and encouraging their milkmen to actively cultivate relationships with customers, the probability of their accomplishing this is greatly increased.

Another factor which contributes to the need for cultivation is the continuing exodus of customers from home delivery to supermarkets. This puts distributors in the position of having to conduct, at best, a holding operation. Because of this, many distributors offer incentives, usually in the form of some sort of commission, to their milkmen to solicit new customers. They are required, at minimum, to replace each customer they lose with a comparable new customer. Thus, under the conditions described above, milkmen are continually engaged in cultivating relationships at various stages of development, including their inception.

To summarize: Over the last several decades, the home delivery milk business has gone through a considerable decline. This has been brought about by a combination of cultural and technological changes, including suburbanization, the increased availability of the automobile and refrigerator, and the decreased perishability of dairy products—all of which have contributed to the increased convenience of the grocery store, especially the supermarket, as a place from which to purchase milk and other dairy products. To make matters worse for the home delivery milkman, the efficiency of the supermarket occasions a price differential which is decidedly to his disadvantage. In response to these conditions, retail distributors in many parts of the country have altered their operating procedures in such a manner that the milkman's job has been extensively changed. Routing procedures—time and frequency of delivery—have been changed, which of course changes the structural routine of the job. But, more importantly, the essence of the job itself has been radically altered. A job which at one time involved very little customer contact has been transformed into a job in which cultivation of customer relationships is an essential task.

Situationally Specific Factors

The conditions in the context within which I made my observations were very similar to those I have described as fairly typical throughout the country. Population density in the area varied from moderately dense (housing tracts) to sparse (farms and ranches), with most sections being somewhere between. Supermarkets were prevalent in the area, and a price differential existed, made manditory by law, with the supermarket price being several cents per quart less than the home delivery price. In addition to competing with supermarkets and other grocery stores, home delivery distributors in the area were compelled to compete rather intensely with one another. There were seven companies, of various sizes, competing for business in an area with only about 275,000 persons, most of whom patronized supermarkets for their dairy products.

In addition, the physical terrain in the area was notably hilly, with approximately half the residences located on hillsides. This slowed delivery time to such an extent that route sizes were significantly affected. This, in combination with the relatively sparse population density, ruled out the formation of compact routes, so a high rate of sales per customer was necessary. And, this, as shown previously, engenders a need for milkmen to actively cultivate customer relationships.

In addition to the foregoing factors, which applied equally to all the home delivery distributors in the area, the distributor for whom I worked utilized several operating procedures which also promoted cultivation of customer relationships by his drivers.[9] They were given responsibility for credit decisions (i.e., who was to get credit and to what extent) and for the distribution of bills and collection of payments. They were also given responsibility for preserving the size of their routes, so that it was necessary for them to routinely seek new customers. These tasks and how they were carried out will be discussed in the following sections.

The aforementioned factors combined made cultivation of relationships with customers imperative for the drivers with whom I worked. To keep their jobs they had to maintain profit-producing routes. To accomplish this, it was necessary to actively initiate and maintain relationships with large numbers of customers and potential customers.

CULTIVATING CUSTOMER RELATIONSHIPS

Learning Cultivating Tactics

Sharing experiences was a daily occurrence with my co-workers. Each workday was followed by a "rap session" which customarily took place in a coffee shop adjacent to the dairy plant. During these sessions, various drivers discussed experiences they had on their routes—unusual events, conversations, problems, and so forth. In addition to being an important source of information for me, these conversations served as extemporaneous training sessions for novice milkmen. In these sessions, new milkmen learned many of the cultivating tactics they needed in order to conduct their routes properly. The "break-in" period given new drivers consisted chiefly of training in the instrumental aspects of the job, such as driving a truck, keeping the route books in order, "working a load," and so forth. This training period lasted only one or two weeks. During this time, novices were concerned mostly with such things as finding the customers' homes, not dropping milk bottles, avoiding unfriendly dogs, and the like. Very little time could be used for teaching cultivating techniques. Thus, cultivating techniques were usually acquired by participating in the daily rap sessions and through trial and error.

This learning took place gradually over a period of several months, and much of it was assimilated with little awareness on the part of the drivers. Thus, the extent to which they were cognizant of the fact that they were manipulating, persuading, and so forth was minimal. I mention this to avoid leaving the impression that they saw themselves as game players, consciously employing tactics and strategies. At certain times, however, they did become aware of the manipulative aspects of their job—particularly when a relationship became problematic, and the need for remedial action was evident. This awareness also emerged when a relationship took a dramatic turn for the better, which was usually attributed to expertise in "handling" customers.[10] Nevertheless, cultivation was so much a part of the drivers' jobs that it was generally performed almost automatically.

Likewise, it is also necessary to emphasize that cultivating was not always successful, its exact extent of success is difficult to ascertain. Customers may have agreed to receive service, increase their orders, terminate their patronage, and so forth for reasons unrelated to the cultivating activities of milkmen. An almost unavoidable effect of my discussion here is that the drivers will appear to be more successful than they probably were.

The cultivating activities of the drivers were organized around three tasks—acquiring new customers, selling "by-products" (products other than milk), and collecting payments. In the course of realizing these tasks, a number of different techniques were used. The acquisition of new customers required the employment of different techniques than did sales and collections, therefore it will be discussed separately. Following this, I will discuss several "decultivating" techniques, employed when a driver wanted to discourage the development of a relationship or, under extreme circumstances, terminate one.

Acquiring New Customers

The task of obtaining new customers involved three distinguishable kinds of techniques, used at three different stages: (1) detecting techniques, used to ferret out potential customers; (2) soliciting techniques, used to procure customers; (3) trust-inducing tactics, used to establish solidarity in new relationships.

DETECTING TECHNIQUES

As I mentioned previously, the distributor for whom I worked required his drivers to maintain, if not increase, the size of their routes. Each driver usually lost five or ten customers per month, although this number varied according to time of year.[11] This number was great enough to make it necessary for drivers to routinely seek new customers. As an incentive, they were given a "bonus" for each new customer they obtained.

Because of the variety of other activities required to operate a route, little time was available to canvass for new customers, so the drivers used several techniques which enabled them to minimize the amount of "route time" they spent in this search.

A driver was not restricted to canvassing only for his route. One driver could "sign up" a customer who would be served by another driver and still receive a bonus. Therefore, it was standard practice for drivers, particularly new drivers, to canvass among their friends, neighbors, and relatives. This would not necessarily increase the size of one's own route, but it would increase the size of one's paycheck, and gain the approval of the route supervisor. This was pretty much a one-time tactic, as the drivers were generally reluctant to ask the same persons more than once or twice.

Another, but seldom used, technique was to ask customers for "leads" among their friends, relatives, and neighbors. This was usually asked only of customers to whom one felt close. This precaution was taken to avoid the risk of offending an existing customer and thereby losing him.

The above two techniques were not generally relied upon for replacing lost customers. Most drivers used two general techniques which could be carried out in the course of running their routes. The first involved getting to know utility installers (e.g., telephone, gas, and electric) who worked in the general area of one's route. These persons had knowledge of what homes were being vacated and what homes were being newly occupied. They ordinarily gave this information to milkmen who were on a friendly basis with them, enabling drivers to get "good leads" with very little time consumed.

The second detecting technique which could be employed "on the route" involved watching for moving vans. Whenever a moving van was seen, drivers stopped and asked whether the party was moving in or out of the house. If they were moving in, he either gave his sales pitch or set a time to talk with the new resident at a later date. If the home was being vacated, the driver simply kept an eye on it until a new resident moved in.

SOLICITING TECHNIQUES

Once good leads were obtained, the drivers had to somehow convince the potential customers to become actual customers.

This was not a particularly easy task, because of the aforementioned price differential. In addition to this differential, a charge of three cents was imposed for each delivery, regardless of the amount delivered. The price differential and delivery charge were undoubtedly the factors most often mentioned by potential customers when declining patronage, and, for the drivers, these were the most difficult to surmount, as they were governed by law.[12] Thus, soliciting techniques most often involved overcoming these price obstacles. The techniques most often used to accomplish (or at least attempt to accomplish) this were "personalizing" and "dealing."[13]

Personalizing. Personalizing consisted of offering a potential customer personalized service which would supposedly make up for the higher cost of home delivery. Such service consisted of such things as entering the customer's house and placing the order in the refrigerator (referred to by the drivers as a "reefer serve"), billing at optional intervals (anywhere from daily to monthly), maintaining an order at a previously designated size,[14] and so forth. In general, personalizing consisted of performing any service a driver felt worthwhile to acquire and keep the patronage of a customer.

The personalizing sales pitch usually consisted of conceding to the potential customer that one's products were of the same general type and quality as those found in grocery stores and that the prices were a bit higher, but maintaining that one's personal service was very much worth receiving. When giving my personalizing sales pitch, I usually emphasized that, once the proper size of the order was established, the customer would never again have to be concerned with purchasing dairy products. I would build her[15] order to whatever level she desired so that she could avoid having to "run to the store" just to get milk. I usually pointed out that the extra trips to the store which she most certainly had been making, aside from being inconvenient, were expensive and time-consuming. And in addition to transportation costs, people usually purchased several other items which they may not otherwise have purchased. I added that this was known and encouraged by store owners, who usually placed dairy products in the back of their stores so that customers would have to walk down aisles filled with food just to pick up a quart of milk. This encouraged impulse buying. I then emphasized that, by taking my service, they could avoid this "trap." Most of my co-workers reported using similar versions of this sales pitch.

Personalizing was a technique which was also used on potential customers who had objections other than price to receiving home delivery. Many persons, for example, objected to home delivery because they worked during the day and were afraid their order might spoil if left outside all day. This objection was easily overcome by offering to leave the order in an insulated box with ice or by offering reefer service.[16]

Dealing. Dealing was ordinarily used only if personalizing failed, and only if the potential customer's would be large enough to warrant its use. It was used regularly by most drivers, but in varying amounts.

Dealing consisted simply of offering a customer a reduction in price. This price reduction took one of several forms. Most drivers preferred giving their "deals" a free quart of milk, pound of butter, half-gallon of ice cream, or whatever at specified intervals. Deals carried out in this manner were easier to cover up than other types of deals. To cover up this type of deal, all a driver needed to do was "dump" the product which was given away. Dumping consisted of claiming the product had gone sour or had been damaged. This allowed the driver to balance his books without taking the loss himself.

Other forms of dealing included reducing the price of specific products and eliminating the delivery charge. These deals were more difficult to cover up because they involved "juggling" the books. Deals could not show on a customer's bill, so drivers were required to hide them. A number of methods were used to accomplish this. Most of them are much too complex to describe briefly, so I shall describe only the most commonly used one.

This method involved hiding deals in daily cash. Drivers acquired five or ten dollars each day from nonregular cash customers. These customers were not entered into the route book, so a driver could adjust the amount of cash he claimed, so long as he dumped enough products to balance his books properly. Drivers kept track of their losses (the amount of money lost on deals) throughout the day, subtracted this amount from their cash, and dumped enough products to make up the difference.

Dealing was implicitly encouraged by the route supervisor, although it was expected to be kept within certain limits. The amount of dealing a particular driver engaged in could be roughly ascertained by the amount of dumping he did. Drivers who dumped more or less than what was considered to be normal were usually warned that they were dumping too much or not enough, which, translated, meant they were either dealing too much or too little. Aside from this, dealing activities were seldom referred to, except among the drivers. The drivers were fully aware that they were expected to deal, and they were expected to do it in such a way that it was hidden from the route supervisor, as well as from state inspectors. Dealing thus had to be accomplished completely from memory, with drivers remembering who they were dealing with and the type and amount of each deal. Nothing could be written down, even in coded form, because it would increase the risk of being caught.

DEVELOPING MUTUAL TRUST

Once a driver had gained the patronage of a new customer, it was essential for him to establish a relationship of mutual trust. His primary concern regarding trust of the customer was credit. He needed to be reasonably sure that the customer would pay her bill. The customer's trust of him often occurred with no action on his part, due apparently to the fact that a certain amount of trust is intrinsic to the role of milkman. Customers seemed to be generally aware that milkmen are easily traceable,[17] and they are ordinarily bonded.

However, some customers demonstrated mistrust, particularly concerning the possibility that their milkman might cheat them either by overcharging them or by charging them for items which they did not purchase. Such customers often kept day-to-day itemized accounts of the products they purchased, along with the prices at which they had been advertised. When they received their bill they compared it against this itemized list to check for discrepancies.

Other customers expressed mistrust regarding the freshness of the products they were receiving. These customers would not accept their milkman's word that the products were fresh. Some insisted on being shown how to translate the "date codes" imprinted on the cartons of most dairy products. These codes give the dump date—the date after which products are not to be sold. This information, combined with knowledge of the "carry over time" (the length of time a product is allowed to remain "on the truck") of a product, allowed them to ascertain how fresh a product was.

Customers who displayed what was perceived as mistrust were handled very carefully, because of fear that they would terminate service over the slightest misunderstanding. This occurred frequently enough to be considered a problem which should be guarded against.

Whether or not actions such as those described above were in fact motivated by mistrust is not altogether clear. Other motives may have been involved. For example, itemized lists may have been kept by some customers for budgeting purposes. Or refusal by customers to provide their milkman with a key may merely have been a convenient way of refusing reefer service. However, the importance of this is that drivers sensed such actions to be manifestations of mistrust and acted accordingly.

The drivers also had reason to cultivate trust with customers who displayed no outward signs of mistrust. It was efficacious for a driver to establish his trustworthiness before he attempted to advance a relationship to a more familiar level. Failing to do so sometimes proved to be unfortunate. I had several experiences, for instance, in which customers terminated their patronage when I attempted to make them reefer serves. They expressed considerable displeasure at my suggestion that they provide me with a key to their houses, which they apparently perceived as an attempt to set up a theft. Until I attempted to make them "reefer serves," I had had very little contact with these customers and they thus had little basis upon which to judge my trustworthiness.

It was a general policy of most of the drivers to go out of their way to display trustworthiness—as an insurance measure. Occasions commonly arose in which this projected trustworthiness was beneficial, such as when bills were added incorrectly or prices were inadvertently misquoted. When customers discovered such things, they often confronted their milkmen with the discrepancy. If they trusted him, they would be apt to take his word that the inconsistency was unintentional.

We see then, that a number of factors made trust cultivation an expedient task. Such cultivation was necessary—sometimes even critically so—for customers who displayed mistrust, and it was applied as an insurance measure to those customers who displayed no outward signs of mistrust.

Trust-inducing tactics. In the course of trust-cultivating, the drivers employed several trust-inducing tactics. These tactics fall suitably into four general categories, which for convenience I will call "the sincerity act," "contrived disclosure," "situational mitigation," and "accentuated honesty."

The sincerity act: The sincerity act was a carefully expressed demeanor. It consisted merely of presenting one's self in a pleasant, straightforward manner which implied confidence and trustworthiness. The sincerity act is not, of course, used exclusively by milkmen. It is employed by just about all persons who deal directly with customers. It has, in fact, been used to excess—enough so that it carries with it the risk of backfiring. If not practiced with the proper amount of reservation, it may be perceived as an indicator of insincerity—the opposite of what it is intended to convey.[18] Many customers disclosed to me in conversation that they thought that one or another of my "relief drivers"[19] acted "phony," "deceitful," and the like.

Most of the drivers recognized the danger in acting too nice and made attempts to counteract the possibility of leaving such an impression, through use of the contrived disclosure tactic. This tactic added substance to the sincerity act.

Contrived disclosure: Contrived disclosure consisted of disclosing, at opportune times, what was implied to be "insider" information. The kind of information offered was not general knowledge, but, on the other hand, it was not as confidential as it was implied to be. The most commonly employed contrived disclosure concerned the date code imprinted on the carton of most dairy products. Although the meaning of this code was not commonly known, it was not intended to be guarded information. It functioned to let the retailer know when unsold products were likely to go bad. Many customers, though, seemed to have the impression that it was information which was intentionally being hidden from them. By voluntarily disclosing the method for translating the code, the drivers could imply that, although distributors and processors might sometimes be less than trustworthy ("after all, they are businessmen"), this particular milkman could be trusted.

Another contrived disclosure that was commonly used to gain the confidence of customers concerned the source of "by-products" (i.e., cottage cheese, yogurt, ice cream, cheese, and so forth). Many of the by-products sold by milkmen in this area were processed by the same company, although they were packaged differently, using the names of the various companies. By disclosing this to unaware customers in a confiding manner, a driver could, again, hopefully gain the trust of a customer.

The type of information which was disclosed was not particularly important. The important thing was that it appear to the customer as special information—something about which few people knew. The driver then appeared to be confiding in the customer, which implied that his loyalty resided with her rather than elsewhere.

Situational mitigation: Situational mitigation was employed primarily with customers who displayed outward signs of mistrust. It consisted of taking direct measures to alleviate the grounds for mistrust. It was commonly used with customers who seemed to be unusually sensitive about the possibility of being cheated. I had one customer, for instance, who continually accused me of overcharging her or adding up her weekly bill incorrectly. The amount involved was never more than a few cents, so I always reimbursed her, with apologies, for whatever amount she claimed to have lost. But the problem occurred with such frequency that she eventually began to imply that I was trying to cheat her. I was afraid that she might terminate her patronage, so I confronted her with a solution. I gave her a mimeographed price list (provided by the company) of all products I sold. I then suggested that, each delivery, I leave a list of the products which she ordered along with the price which she was charged for each item. She could then compare this list with what she thought to be correct, and if a discrepancy was found we could work it out the following delivery. Never again did the problem arise. In fact, several months later she told me not to bother leaving the list any more and apologized for having caused me so much bother. I had, apparently, successfully eliminated the grounds for her mistrust of me.

A similar direct approach was used with customers who expressed concern over the freshness of the products they were receiving. Customers who exhibited such concern were usually told where the date code was on the various products, and how to translate it. This allowed them to ascertain the freshness of the products delivered to them, without having to rely on their milkman's word.[20]

In any case, situational mitigation allowed a driver to directly eliminate grounds for mistrust. By doing this, he could generally establish a relationship on a more stable foundation and, if desired, proceed with further cultivation.

Accentuated honesty: Another commonly used trust-inducing tactic was accentuated honesty. This tactic was used whenever a situation arose in which a driver could overtly display honesty. One such situation commonly arose when drivers inadvertently caused minor damage to fences, shrubs, and so forth while maneuvering their trucks. Often such damage was minor enough that it would likely go unnoticed. However, situations such as this could easily and safely be used to display honesty. For instance, I once backed my truck into a customer's picket fence and damaged one picket. Though I could have ignored the damage, as several nearby pickets had been previously damaged by someone else, I notified the customer. She laughed and said that she probably would not even have noticed it. I insisted that I personally pay for it (the company would have paid for it), but she thanked me for my honesty and refused my offer. This display of honesty appeared to have been beneficial, because prior to this time, this customer had purchased only milk, but, shortly after this event, she began regularly purchasing "extras."

Another type of situation in which honesty could be accentuated is brought about by billing errors. Monthly bills were sometimes added incorrectly.[21] If the error is large, customers usually notice it very quickly. But small errors are often overlooked. Whenever a driver discovered such an error, he was, again, presented with a convenient opportunity to accentuate his honesty.

Predicting credit trustworthiness. As I mentioned previously, the drivers were concerned with developing mutual trust. They needed not only to convince customers of their trustworthiness, but also to ascertain the credit trustworthiness of customers. They were given responsibility for determining who was to receive what kind of credit—ranging from daily to monthly. It was necessary for them to ascertain the trustworthiness of particular customers within the first several deliveries. They had, especially, to guard against two types of customers—deadbeats and skippers.[22] Deadbeats were customers who ran up large bills and then refused to pay them. Skippers were customers who ran up large bills and then changed their residence without notifying their milkmen and without leaving a forwarding address with the post office, utility company, or any other agency through which they could be traced.

The drivers used certain commonsense indicators to aid them in predicting the trustworthiness of a customer. They first of all took notice of the general appearance of the neighborhood—was it a good neighborhood or a bad one? Second, they noted the general appearance of the house—was it nice or was it crummy? On the first delivery, they attempted to contact the customer. If she answered the door, attempts were made to strike up a conversation. This served two purposes. In the course of conversation, useful information, such as the husband's occupation, might be disclosed. Also, it might result in an invitation to step inside the door. Once inside, the general appearance of the inside of the house could be noted—was it carefully kept and nicely furnished or not?

These indicators served to aid a driver in deciding what kind of a "risk" a particular customer was. A carelessly kept house in a bad neighborhood indicated (supposedly) a credit risk. If it was decided that a particular customer was a potential risk, attempts were made to get more information. The customer was contacted, either in person or by telephone, and asked questions regarding the husband's occupation, place of employment, and so forth. The driver usually explained, apologetically, that the company required him to get such information. This relieved him of personal responsibility and lessened the risk of irritating the customer.

Customers who were defined as low risks were given a choice of what interval they would be billed at. Those who were defined as risky were usually extended weekly credit. Those who were thought to be very risky were told that they would have to pay cash each delivery—at least for awhile. After several weeks, the driver usually offered them weekly credit. If this presented no problems, eventually they were offered monthly credit. This method of gradual progression enabled the driver to keep the customer's bill from "getting out of hand," and it allowed him to acquire more information which would hopefully allow him to more closely establish the customer's trustworthiness. It also eliminated the risk of making a customer angry by withdrawing credit which had already been extended.

Sales and Collections

Aside from acquiring new customers and developing trust, selling by-products and collecting bills were the tasks around which most of the drivers' cultivating activities were organized. These were the most essential tasks, and the ones which consumed the most time. The techniques employed in carrying out these two tasks were essentially the same. Most of the drivers found it best to manage the two tasks indirectly, through certain subtle cultivating techniques. The hard sell approach carried with it a high risk of offending customers and therefore was seldom used.[23] The most commonly used techniques were what, for convenience, I will refer to as "nurturing pseudo friendship," and "effecting obligation."

NURTURING PSEUDO FRIENDSHIP

The aim of this maneuver was simply to establish oneself on friendly terms with customers. The object was not to become personal friends (although that sometimes did occur), but merely to become well liked. It was assumed that a customer would express her regard for a well-liked milkman by purchasing extras, paying her bill promptly, and so forth.

The most crucial activities in a budding relationship were conversations and accepting an offer for a cup of coffee. They both tended to promote relationships. Thus, when an appropriate opportunity arose, a driver would strike up a "friendly" conversation with a customer, usually on a topic which seemed to interest her—her children, her hobby, or whatever. The first conversation usually opened the door for further ones. A driver

could promote this by, if possible, somehow referring to the
previous conversation when he made his next delivery. This
indicated that he remembered the conversation and enjoyed it.
After one or two conversations (if not sooner), a customer
usually offered the milkman a cup of coffee, which, if he
wished to nurture the relationship, he accepted. If things
progressed normally, the offer for coffee became routine,
although because of time limitations it was not always accepted.
When the relationship reached this stage, it was considered a
successful one. Such relationships were called "coffee stops."

When nurturing friendly relationships, the driver attempted
to leave the impression that the customer involved was one of
his "favorite" customers, which may or may not have been the
case. Each driver usually had forty or fifty favorite customers.

EFFECTING OBLIGATION

The aim of this technique was to somehow instill in
customers a sense of obligation or indebtedness. It was, again,
assumed that customers would reciprocate through increased
sales and prompt bill payments.[24] Effecting obligation was
accomplished, ordinarily, in two different ways—through offering "specials," and through performing "favors."

Specials. Each week the company offered specials to all
customers. On Monday and Tuesday, a list of three or four
items was left with each customer's order. The items on the list
were sold, for one week, at a reduced price. Often a customer
would express concern that an item she wanted was not on
special. This offered an opportunity for the driver to promote a
sense of indebtedness in the customer. He could inform her
that, "because he was in a good mood," or some other such
expression, he would give her a "special" on the item she
wanted. If the customer had a large family and was therefore a
potentially big customer, he might even offer to make the
special permanent (i.e., charge her at a reduced price whenever
she bought the product).

Another type of special was what the drivers called a "freezer pack." Customers who had large freezers and large families were offered freezer packs. A freezer pack consisted of eleven or twelve half-gallons of ice cream for the regular price of ten half-gallons.

In general, specials were usually offered on high-volume sales, such as freezer packs, and on expensive items, such as large blocks of cheese. This minimized the loss incurred by granting the special, and also offered an opportunity to increase the sales of items which were otherwise difficult to sell. Permanent specials were very much like deals, the main difference being in their intent. Deals were offered to maintain the patronage of customers, whereas specials were offered to enhance the solidarity of relationships. Specials, like deals, were covered up by dumping.

Favors. Another way of incurring obligation in customers was to perform favors for them. A wide variety of favors was performed by the drivers. The most common ones included such things as mailing letters, turning on ovens for absent housewives, doing minor automobile repairs, and so forth. It was also common for a customer to ask a driver if he knew of anyone who wanted to buy a used bicycle, automobile, washing machine, and so on. Often a buyer could be found among the driver's other customers. Searching for a buyer was sometimes a bother, but if one could be found the payoff was usually sufficient to have made the effort worthwhile. I sold several items in this manner, and the customers involved expressed their gratitude in the way which I had hoped for—by increasing their sales. Similar experiences were commonly reported by other drivers.

The above cultivating techniques (nurturing pseudo-friendship and effecting obligation) were beneficial in other ways than just those described above. They allowed the drivers not only to enhance sales and collections, but also to manipulate customers in other advantageous ways. The drivers were expected to maintain a balance between what they sold and what they collected in payments during any given month. If a driver sold

$5,000 worth of products one month he was expected to collect at least $5,000 in payments the following month. Those who accomplished this were said to have "collected out." Drivers who collected out were given a bonus.

Collecting out was rather difficult to accomplish regularly, because customers did not always pay their bills promptly. This meant that a driver might fall short of collecting out one month and greatly excede it the next month. Thus, although the credit on his route was "clean," he was not always able to achieve his bonus. However, if a driver had a pool of customers who held him in high regard or felt a sense of obligation toward him, he could better his chances of collecting out. During months in which it appeared that he might come up short, he could ask these customers to please pay their bill before the end of the month, if they had not already done so—explaining to them that he needed more payments to achieve his bonus. On the other hand, if he had already collected out, he could ask these customers to please not pay their bill until after the first of the next month, which would help him to collect out the following month. Some customers became so accustomed to this that they always consulted their milkman before paying their bill.

Sales could be manipulated in a similar manner. Drivers were expected to be able to outsell their relief drivers. If a relief driver had a "$200 day" (i.e., sold $200 worth of products) on, say, a Wednesday, it was expected that the regular driver would have sold more than that on the previous Wednesday. The assumption was that regular drivers knew their customers better than relief drivers and should therefore be able to sell more to them. Regular drivers were ordinarily admonished when they were outsold by a relief driver. To avoid this, drivers asked those customers whom they felt they had the confidence of not to purchase extras from their relief driver if they were able to wait until the next delivery. This lessened the probability that they would be outsold.

Decultivating Techniques

When conducting their routes, the drivers were hampered by

a critical shortage of time. They delivered to anywhere from 100 to 200 customers each day. Because of this, the amount of time they could spend cultivating any one relationship was severely limited. This being the case, they ordinarily gauged the amount of time they spent cultivating a particular relationship according to what they estimated to be its payoff potential. More time was alloted for customers with high payoff potential than was alloted for customers with low payoff potential—or at least this was the ideal.[25] However, customers themselves often attempted to initiate closer relationships with the drivers. If such relationships appeared to have low payoff potential, they somehow had to be inhibited.

INHIBITING CONDUCT

As I mentioned previously, two activities—conducting conversations and drinking coffee with customers—were crucial in budding relationships. Encouraging these activities could promote a relationship; discouraging them could inhibit a relationship. In accordance with this, drivers discouraged these activities when carrying out low-yield relationships. They accomplished this by conducting themselves in a designated manner. When in the presence of low-yield customers they maintained a pleasant demeanor, so as not to appear rude, but always acted as if they were in a hurry, whether or not they actually were. This gave them an account for breaking conversations short and also provided them with a convenient excuse for not accepting a cup of coffee. By conducting themselves in this manner, they could discourage the development of a relationship without offending the customer.

However, this tactic sometimes failed, and a relationship got out of hand. When this occurred, a driver had two alternatives—coping the best he could or terminating the relationship. About the only way to cope with such relationships was to deal with each enounter separately. When delivering to these customers, the drivers usually approached the house very quietly, sometimes parking their truck a short distance down the street. By doing this, the hope was that they might be able to avoid contact with the customer. If this failed, they simply gave whatever account they could think of to break the ensuing conversation short.

Occasionally, a relationship got so far out of hand, that a driver decided it would be best to terminate it. This was usually done only with customers who habitually consumed excessive amounts of time. Customers who were terminated were those who persisted in carrying out fifteen- or twenty-minute (sometimes even more) conversations each delivery. Terminating customers was strictly forbidden by the route supervisor (except for credit reasons), so the drivers utilized tactics for accomplishing this without notice.

TERMINATING TACTICS

In general, terminating tactics consisted of provoking a customer to discontinue patronage on what she thought was her own initiative. If this could be accomplished, a driver could rid himself of a problem relationship without incurring the wrath of the route supervisor. The two most commonly employed terminating tactics were "the holdover tactic," and "the incompetance tactic."

The Holdover tactic. The most commonly employed terminating tactic was executed by intentionally delivering bad products to the customer. To do this, a driver would "hold over" a product, usually a carton of milk, on his truck for about a week or so before delivering it. By this time the product was on the verge of turning sour, but not sour enough that the ploy would be discovered. This was done every several deliveries until, hopefully, the customer terminated service. The advantage of this tactic was that it alleviated the milkman of responsibility.

The incompetence tactic. Another common tactic, sometimes employed when the holdover tactic failed, was the incompetence tactic. In using this tactic, a driver intentionally displayed clumsiness, stupidity, and general inefficiency. To manage this, he did such things as accidentally breaking milk bottles in inappropriate places (on the front porch, kitchen floor, and so on), inadvertently foregetting to deliver part of an order, delivering unordered products, incorrectly adding bills, and so forth. This tactic was ordinarily employed only as a last resort, as it carried with it the risk of provoking the route supervisor, particularly if the customer telephoned the dairy office to complain of the milkman's incompetence.

DISCUSSION

The foregoing analysis, although focused primarily on the milkman-customer relationship, offers a conceptual framework which, I believe, would be valuable in the analysis of other types of service relationships. The cultivating process is clearly present in many such relationships (for examples see Davis, 1959; Gold, 1964; Habenstein, 1962; Whyte, 1946).[26] The limited glance afforded by this short analysis of the milkman-customer relationship is not sufficient to develop, with any depth, the pertinent dimensions of the general process of cultivating. However, if this framework were employed in further research on service relationships, these dimensions could be developed, and a more formal theory concerning cultivating could be forwarded. Despite the inability to accomplish this from the foregoing analysis, several dimensions of cultivating—particularly regarding the structural conditions according to which the need for it varies—are evident in this context which can serve as general hypothesis for further research. I shall, then, briefly discuss some aspects of cultivating as it relates to service relationships in general—keeping in mind that what I say is largely hypothetical and certainly incomplete.

One important aspect of cultivating, it seems, is reciprocity. When the milkmen discussed in this paper employed what I previously referred to as nurturing pseudo-friendship and effecting obligation, they were capitalizing on what Gouldner

(1960) referred to as "the norm of reciprocity." These tactics were employed with the expectation that customers would reciprocate friendship, specials, and favors by increasing their sales, paying their bills at the proper time, and so forth. Similar tactics are employed in other types of service relationships. Gasoline service station operators, for instance, often loan tools, give free advice, and so forth to certain customers with the expectation that the customers will reciprocate by receiving and paying for the full range of services offered at the station.

Another apparent dimension of cultivating is trust—both its development and its maintenance. A very important aspect of the milkman-customer relationship, as we have seen, is the development of trust. Trust seems to be particularly important in service relationships which involve expertise. Laymen generally are at the mercy of expert servicers. Television repairmen, for instance, can easily cheat customers, as customers have no basis upon which to judge the service of the repairmen. They have no way of ascertaining whether a repairman did the services he claimed to have done, whether he did them properly, and so forth. Customers generally are aware of this. This puts the expert in the position of having to display trustworthiness in the course of carrying out his services. Even experts such as medical doctors, who are accorded a high amount of role trust, must behave in a manner which confirms their trustworthiness (a matter of trust maintenance; see Freidson, 1961).

The structural source of cultivating as it relates to service relationships is what could be called "contextual power asymmetry."[27] Power in service relationships is contextual in that it ordinarily applies only within the servicing context.[28] In other types of relationships, such as marriage, power may be more pervasive.

I use the term "power asymmetry" to refer to the balance of power in a relationship. Quite simply, a relationship which is characterized by power asymmetry is one in which one party, for any number of reasons, exercises more control over the course of the relationship (in this case, within the servicing context) than does the other party. The milkman-customer relationship, for example, is one which is characterized, at least initially, by acute power asymmetry.

The balance of power in a relationship can be altered through the use of cultivating techniques. In this sense, cultivating is a leveling mechanism. The milkman clearly uses it as such. Through the use of cultivating techniques, he is able to effectively increase the amount of control he exercises in relationships with his customers. In some instances, particularly those in which he has successfully nurtured pseudo-friendship and effected obligation, he is able to accomplish near symmetry.

The most basic source of power asymmetry in service relationships, it seems, is simple supply and demand.[29] If a service is low in demand and high in supply, as is the case with the home delivery milk business, power asymmetry will likely be acute, and the need for cultivation will, accordingly, be high. Likewise, as demand increases and supply decreases, power asymmetry will likely become less acute and, accordingly, the need for cultivation on the part of the servicer will decrease, eventually reaching a point where power symmetry is reversed and the servicee, rather than the servicer, is compelled to cultivate.[30]

If this observation is correct, we would expect that medical doctors, for instance, would be required to spend a minimal amount of time cultivating relationships with patients. This is not to say that they would be able to refrain completely from cultivating. Freidson's (1961) discussion of doctor-patient relationships clearly shows that doctors are not exempt from having to use cultivating techniques. However, it is quite evident that doctor-patient relationships involve much less cultivating than do milkman-customer relationships. According to Freidson's findings, the cultivating activities of doctors seem to consist primarily of attempts to convince patients of the wisdom of their diagnoses and prescriptions—which, as I suggested before, seems to be a matter of trust maintenance.

The relationship between cultivating and supply and demand is particularly evident when a service occupation is on either the incline or the decline. The occupation of milkman is quite obviously on the decline. The economic demand for his service, which at one time was a necessity, has steadily declined over the last several decades. At the same time, through the rise of the supermarket, the supply of servicers has effectively increased. Thus, the milkman's past dominance over the retail milk business has been lost. And this, as was previously shown, is one of the chief conditions which gave rise to the need for milkmen to engage in cultivating activities.

The relationship between cultivating and supply and demand in an inclining service occupation is evident in Habenstein's (1962) analysis of the ascent of the American funeral director. Previous to the rise of the funeral director, the various tasks associated with preparing and burying the dead were handled by a wide range of occupations, including "nurses, sextons, cabinetmakers, livery stable operators, and other factotums" (Habenstein, 1962: 228). The demand for death-related services was high, but the supply and variety of servicers was also high. Thus, to establish themselves as a discernible occupation, funeral directors had to create a psychological demand for *their* service. In other words, they had to convince their potential customers that the way in which they carried out death-related services was preferable to other ways. This they accomplished, essentially, through cultivating.[31] Their success is well evidenced by the fact that modern Americans would be horrified (or highly amused) at the suggestion that they take their dead relatives to a cabinetmaker for preparation and burial.

Another factor which seems to affect the extent to which cultivating is associated with a particular service occupation is relative expertise. High-expertise service occupations, particularly the professions, seem to involve a lower amount of cultivating activity than low-expertise occupations. Cultivating in such relationships seems to be, as I suggested previously, directed mainly at trust maintenance, for at least two reasons.

First, as Caplow (1954: 170) pointed out regarding the professions, the supply of expert servicers tends to be kept at a relatively low level through occupational controls over such things as eligibility requirements and training. This effectively increases the demand (in relation to the supply) for the services of the limited number of "legitimate" expert servicers.

Secondly, high-expertise service occupations, again particularly the professions, tend to develop "professional ethics" which severely restrict those kinds of activities to which I have referred as cultivating.

The above general discussion is unavoidably sketchy and in no way conclusive. The general dimensions which I have alluded to were advanced primarily as hypotheses, although they were suggested by the empirical instance of the milkman. Verification of the extent to which these are the pertinent dimension is contingent upon application of this conceptual framework in the analysis of other types of service relationships.

NOTES

1. Although Goffman was referring to expert services, his statement clearly can be extended to include nonexpert services.

2. I use the term power, in this context, to refer to the ability to guide the course of a relationship. In the milkman-customer relationship, the customer possesses more power—i.e., in the end is able to exert more control over the direction of the relationship—than the milkman, although the extent of this power is alterable. The ultimate source of this power resides in the customer's prerogative to terminate the relationship with less cause and at less cost than the milkman.

3. For a discussion of relative power symmetry in social relationships see Glaser (forthcoming).

4. This information is obtained from E. Linwood Tipton (1971: 118) an economist with the Milk Industry Foundation.

5. Low-consumption customers are considered, generally, to be those whose families consume less than ten quarts of milk per week.

6. According to Stone (1954), large numbers (28% of his sample) of shoppers (on Chicago's northwest side, in the early 1950s) preferred the personalized service found in "local" stores over the larger variety and lower prices found in large department stores. The factors which accounted for this may also play a part in home delivery customers' decisions to purchase their dairy products from milkmen rather than from supermarkets.

7. Many distributors are both wholesale and retail, but the two types of distribution are ordinarily administered separately from one another.

8. Some customers still prefer early delivery. To accommodate them, many distributors set the "starting time" of their routes around five or six in the morning.

This allows for early delivery to those customers who prefer it and daytime delivery to those who do not.

9. Hereafter I will refer to my former co-workers as "drivers," as that is what they called themselves.

10. When questioned about the manipulative aspects of their job, the drivers were quick to acknowledge that they did employ tactics, strategies, and so forth. They agreed, however, that they did not think much about them—they just "did" them.

11. More customers were lost in the summer, as families change residences more often during that time of year.

12. The law was enforced by a state "board" which was given authority to punish distributors who violated it by imposing fines and so on.

13. The world "dealing" was used by the drivers. The term "personalizing" is my own.

14. This was referred to as "building" and consisted of the milkman making certain a particular number of products was always available to the customer. For instance, if a build order consisted of five quarts of milk, the driver would leave whatever amount was necessary to bring the total amount of milk in the refrigerator up to five quarts, considering what may have been left over from previous deliveries.

15. Hereafter I will refer to customers in the female gender, as with very few exceptions, milkman-customer relationships are between milkmen and females.

16. Most reefer serves gave their milkman a house key, which he placed in his route book next to the customer's billing sheet.

17. For a discussion of trust and traceability, see Henslin (1968).

18. One is reminded here of the common stereotype regarding the "sincerity" of used car salesmen.

19. Relief drivers were drivers who had no regular route. They operated the regular drivers' routes when they were on vacations, days off, and so forth.

20. The date code, if you recall, was used also with the contrived disclosure tactic.

21. Monthly bills were added by office workers. All other bills (semi-monthly, weekly, and so on) were added by the drivers.

22. These terms were used by the drivers.

23. Two of the drivers had reputations as "hard sellers." They both had perpetual trouble with customer relationships, so they were eventually made relief drivers. Relief drivers alternated among five different routes, so they could come in contact with any one customer only once every several weeks. In addition, they were not expected to go out of their way to sell or collect bills. These two factors minimized the risk of their offending customers.

24. For pertinent discussions of reciprocity, see Gouldner (1960) and Mauss (1954).

25. The payoff potential of customers was usually estimated according to family size.

26. Although cultivating as such is not discussed in these studies, the use of cultivating techniques by the cabdriver, apartment building janitor, funeral director, and waitress is evident.

27. The term "power symmetry" is borrowed from Glaser (forthcoming).

28. Goffman (1961: 324) alludes to this in his definition of "personal-service occupation": "A personal-service occupation may be defined, ideally, as one whose

practitioner performs a specialized personal service for a set of individuals where the service requires him to engage in direct personal communication with each of them and where he is not otherwise bound to the person he serves."

29. Demand for a service, as Caplow (1954: 170) noted (regarding professional services), can be either economic or psychological.

30. Black markets and the current marijuana market constitute examples of the latter instance. The most extreme example, I suppose, would be the relationship between narcotic addicts and pushers.

31. The particular techniques which they used to accomplish this are well illustrated by Habenstein and consist generally of their capitalizing on, and to some extent helping to form, the cultural aesthetics of death in America.

REFERENCES

BAUMER, E. F., W. K. BRANDT, R. E. JACOBSON, and F. E. WALKER (1969) "Dimensions of consumer attitude in fluid milk purchases with special reference to doorstep delivery vs. store purchases." Research Bull. 1028, Wooster, Ohio, Agricultural Research and Development Center.

CAPLOW, T. (1954) The Sociology of Work. New York: McGraw-Hill.

DAVIS, F. (1959) "The cabdriver and his fare: facets of a fleeting relationship." Amer. J. of Sociology 65, 2: 158-165.

FREIDSON, E. (1961) "Dilemmas in the doctor-patient relationship," pp. 171-192 in E. Freidson (ed.) Patients' Views of Medical Practice. New York: Russell Sage.

GLASER, B. G. (forthcoming) The Patsy and the Subcontractor.

GOFFMAN, E. (1961) "The medical model and mental hospitalization," pp. 321-386 in Asylums. Garden City, N.Y.: Doubleday.

GOLD, R. L. (1964) "In the basement—the apartment building janitor," in P. L. Berger (ed.) The Human Shape of Work. New York: Macmillan.

GOULDNER, A. W. (1960) "The norm of reciprocity: a preliminary statement." Amer. Soc. Rev. 25 (April): 161-178.

HABENSTEIN, R. W. (1962) "Sociology of occupations: the case of the American funeral director," in A. M. Rose (ed.) Human Behavior and Social Processes. Boston: Houghton Mifflin.

HENSLIN, J. M. (1968) "Trust and the cab driver," pp. 125-158 in M. Truzzi (ed.) Sociology and Everyday Life. Englewood Cliffs, N.J.: Prentice-Hall.

MAUSS, M. (1954) Essay on the Gift. New York: Free Press.

ROADHOUSE, C. and J. HENDERSON (1950) The Market Milk Industry. New York: McGraw-Hill.

STONE, G. P. (1954) "City shoppers and urban identification: observations on the social psychology of city life." Amer. J. of Sociology 60, 1: 36-45.

TIPTON, E. L. (1971) "The vanishing milkman." Futurist (June): 118.

WHYTE, W. F. (1946) "When workers and customers meet," in W. F. Whyte (ed.) Industry and Society. New York: McGraw-Hill.

III. SUPERORDINATION

Superordination is, of course, the other side of subordination. Dixon's report focuses on the superordination of subordinates who are especially recalcitrant—namely, children. McClenahen and Lofland's treatment of bad news in the context of the deputy U.S. Marshal highlights that particular and special problem of superordinates, although, obviously, superordinates are not the only actors who have to manage such a situation.

CAROL DIXON is an advanced graduate student in sociology at the University of California, Davis. Her research interests are in the areas of education, socilization, and small-group processes.

GUIDED OPTIONS AS A PATTERN OF CONTROL IN A HEADSTART PROGRAM

CAROL DIXON

THE ASSEMBLING OF CHILDREN under specialized adult supervision is a ubiquitous feature of American society. And the manner in which such specialized supervision is to be organized is a topic of continuing concern and diatribe. At one extreme are the defenders of conventional and authoritarian organization of these specialized assemblages called classrooms (Bagley, 1907; Bettelheim, 1969). At the other extreme are proponents of permissiveness and various notions of the "open classroom" (Neill, 1960; Kohl, 1969; Rasberry and Greenway, 1970).

Despite much concern and advocacy, relatively little attention has been directed to how educational assemblages of children are in fact organized. This paper is an account of one pattern of organization and control, as observed in a Headstart preschool.

The observed pattern of organization and control will be called the "guided options management strategy." If methods of classroom control are seen as a continuum, with the extremes of an authoritarian system on one end and total permissiveness on the other, guided options may be seen as falling somewhere in the middle. The strategy is not one of prohibiting certain actions or of allowing all actions, but rather one of suggesting or making available alternatives among which the child can choose as replacements for the unacceptable option.

SETTING

The observations reported are drawn from participant observation in a Headstart program in an industrial, West Coast city. The center is located in a black, low-income neighborhood. The children are from three to five years old; there are eight boys and ten girls. All are black except for one boy, who is white.

The head teacher, a young black woman, receives a salary, as does her assistant, a neighborhood mother whose child is in the program. The classroom assistants, who do not come every day and who are not paid, are three neighborhood black women; two white girls; and a white male volunteer who came late in the observation period. A typical session would consist of fourteen children, the head teacher, her assistant, and one or two classroom assistants.

I worked in the program as a classroom assistant three days a week for two months. Notes on events were written up after each session.

ORIENTING: SUGGESTED TECHNIQUES

Volunteers in the program are oriented from their first day with a variety of suggested techniques. The main ones are: (1) diversionary tactics; (2) territorial reassignment; (3) cooperative offers of help; and (4) reminders. All of these are embodied in the initial instruction I received from Rose, the head teacher:

When a child is doing something you don't want him to do, NEVER say "that's bad" or "you're a bad boy" but instead try to distract him. "Would you like to come help me fix the blocks here" [diversionary tactics] or "would you please go into the other room and see if there are any blocks there?" [territorial reassignment] etc. If he leaves toys out, instead of just ordering him to pick them up, offer to help him. "Should I help you put these away now?" [cooperative offers of help] or if he refuses, say, "here, I'll put these away now and next time it will be your turn." Keep track of who's been playing with what and then at clean-up time you can say, "oh Edward, you forgot to take care of your blocks" [reminders].

These tactics may be accompanied by specific gestures, such as holding out a hand to lead the child to his newly assigned territory, or handing him one of the blocks he forgot to put away.

CHILDREN'S RESPONSES

As suggested by Rose's "or if he refuses" remark, the child's response to the initial suggestion will influence further inter-action and possible techniques. There appear to be five main ways in which a child can respond other than accepting the guided option. (1) He may simply *ignore* the caretaker.

Aleisha started pulling books out of the bookshelves and complain-ing, saying she didn't want to hear that old stuff. Mrs. Sloan told her she didn't have to, but asked her what did she do when she first got up? who woke her up or did she get up herself? Aleisha didn't answer but continued to try disrupting the small group by walking around, interrupting, and trying to get a story read instead.

(2) On the other hand, he may *force the situation,* possibly by refusing loudly and deliberately, forcing the teacher to take note of his activities. In the incident above, for example, Aleisha was trying to force the caretaker to notice her at the same time that she was ignoring the caretaker's questions. At other times the refusal is verbal:

As each child came in, I'd ask them if they'd met Dan, he was a new volunteer, tell him their name, then get a name tag and put it on. Sara didn't want one, I tried putting it in a different place, "let's see, would you like it on your pocket? How about the hem of your dress?" etc., all responded to with "NO." "It's only for today, so that Dan can tell who you are, you've met Dan haven't you, so Dan will know who you are?" "NO." She went into the other room with Rose, after a while I went in there; Sara still didn't want a name tag, Rose went through the explanation again, "now let Carol put the name tag on you, it's for Dan, he's the new volunteer, and it's so he can call you by name, otherwise he'll just have to say 'hey you girl,' instead of your name, you want him to call you Sara, don't you?" "NO."

(3) There is also *passive resistance,* used especially in connection with territorial reassignment. The child goes limp, if they want him in the other room, they're going to have to carry him there. Passive resistance can also be used to disrupt orderly activities through sheer delay:

Going back from the park Vivian had sand in her shoes, so first we kept the group waiting while she poured sand out of one and I tied it for her; then we all started off, got to the grassy corner, and she stopped to do the other one. This time she was going to tie it herself, she knew how, what she did was verrry slowwwly put the laces around her ankle, attempt to tie it in back, meanwhile the group was getting way ahead and I knew they were going to have to wait for us at the corner again.

(4) Or the child may move over into *active resistance,* including the use of threats. He may jerk away from the gesture of an offered hand; he may run away; he may kick, squirm, and spit.

Aleisha at one point was getting pretty lively, asked her if she wanted to come work on a puzzle or something with me; she bared her teeth and said "I'll bite you," pretty serious about it too; can't always use lead-by-the hand as management strategy.

In this instance, Aleisha effectively countered her caretaker's combination of diversion and territorial reassignment.

(5) Another response, often connected with cooperative offers of help, is the *smother-with-affection* resistance that Rose warns against:

> One kid will come and hug you around the neck, and then another will want to, and another and another, and pretty soon they're strangling you—it's not fun, not a game, but strangling.

This smother-with-affection resistance can also be used to disrupt teacher-led activities:

> Rose had them jumping, doing jumping jacks, running in place, sitting down on the floor and touching their toes . . . when she sat down, one of the girls immediately held onto her arm, so she couldn't do the exercise, she asked the girl to let go because she couldn't do it, another came and clung to her, too; she eventually stood up again.

HANDLING DISRUPTIVE BEHAVIOR

Obviously these are just possible responses, not invariant ones. But they do occur, and the teacher is then likely to respond with an additional range of tactics for handling this disruptive behavior. I observed six main tactics directed toward managing disruptive behavior. (1) Sometimes *ignoring* the child works:

> Walking back from the park, Tammy and DeeDee were holding Aleisha's hand, and began to dig their nails into her hand, she started crying, they let go and she clung to my hand crying; this was getting a little awkward, I was holding Vivian's coat and her hand; Audrey was semi-wrapped around my leg; and Aleisha on the other hand, and the coat was slipping but I couldn't get free enough to get it more firmly over my arm. . . . Vivian then tried digging her nails into my hand to see if it could hurt, luckily they're short and didn't so I didn't react at all, like I didn't even notice, and she stopped.

Here the smother-with-affection techniques had effectively
disabled the caretaker: she "couldn't get free enough" to
respond physically to Vivian by pulling her hand away. A verbal
request might not have been effective without forcing a scene,
perhaps slipping into authoritarian commands and threats. A
reasonable alternative, which worked this time, was to ignore
the behavior until the child stopped it of her own accord.

(2) At other times, however, the caretaker may attempt to
handle disruptive behavior by *response-demanding* behavior of
her own. For example, when the child ignores the caretaker, she
may simply repeat her suggestion until he answers; or she may
use a response-demanding question, coupled perhaps with a
rhetorical exhortation like "let's get it together."

> As line-up hassles continue, kids keep wandering off, sit down to get
> sand out of their shoes, go back to turtle-thing, Rose becomes more
> insistent. "Now we can't spend so much time lining up, if you can't
> line up we're going to have to spend tomorrow in the building all the
> time and not come here, do you want that, [name]? . . . Do you
> hear me, [name]? . . . Do you understand me, [name]?"

Rose's questions were directed to specific children, and she
waited for each to answer before going on to the next child.

(3) At other times it may be enough to simply suggest a *new
diversion:*

> Meanwhile James F. was careening around on the floor with a big
> wooden truck, trying to run into things, sort of sullen expression on
> his face, mostly trying for attention: first I asked him to please take
> the truck onto the carpet so it wouldn't make so much noise, he
> very carefully didn't hear. Then I asked him if he would like to come
> to our tea party, and he nodded yes and came over and sat down on
> one of the chairs by me.

(4) Especially when faced with situational forcing or active
resistance, the teacher may use the method of *leaving up in the
air,* in which she can postpone resolution or send an "over to
you" to another caretaker:

> Aleisha also keeps tilting her chair, Rose asks her a couple of times
> to get it up to the table, then asks, "Carol, will you help Aleisha get
> her chair up to the table?" so I move it up.

Rose, sitting at the head of the table, was too far away from
Aleisha to do more than ask her to move her chair. Rather than
demanding a response when her requests were ignored, she
turned the situation over to the teacher sitting right beside
Aleisha, using approximately the wording of a cooperative offer
of help. The second teacher was then able to "help" Aleisha
without encountering resistance.

   This technique may fail miserably, however, if the caretakers
don't get their signals straight:

> The fight started I think when Timothy threw some sand in James
> C.' face. . . . Sandi and I could maybe have stopped it better if
> there'd been another supervisor, because then she could have
> watched the other eight children as we kept these two apart until
> they cooled down, but—no other supervisor. And I sort of left it to
> Sandi, as they were over by her, and she probably sort of left it to
> me.

   (5) *Explanation* is another technique which is used frequently. It is sometimes used when a child has rejected the option he
was being guided toward, in an attempt to make him decide
that he wants that option after all. The earlier example of Sara
and the name tag illustrates this use of explanation. It is also
used to soften incidents of deprivation:

> Began to be pushing and hitting and shoving on the slide itself, so I
> took the slide down: "someone is going to get hurt so we aren't
> going to play with this any more today."

It is often used with repetition, explaining over and over until
the child eventually changes his behavior, perhaps out of sheer
boredom:

Asked Wilson if he wanted David to teeter him, Wilson said no, so I
explained to David that Wilson didn't want him to do that, that
Wilson was doing a trick and that then it was Timothy's turn to play
on the slide, he could be after Timothy, along with holding his arm,
keeping him away, explaining twice so he started getting bored with
the long explanation and wandered off.

(6) So far the management techniques described have fit
fairly well with the philosophy of soft control present in the
guided options strategy. Occasionally, however, a more authoritarian tactic is used, that of *seclusion*. It usually occurs when
nothing else has worked and when for some reason it seems
impossible to leave the situation up in the air. Even when used,
it is usually couched in the language of options as a request or
suggestion, although in fact the child's options are extremely
limited at this point. He can either stop what he is doing or he
can wind up in seclusion.

James F. was creating a disturbance in the other room and Rose
brought him into the kitchen to be with her, saying 'if I can't be out
there to be with you, then you come into the kitchen so you can be
with me, sit right there.'

Rose ignored them at first; then when [they] got too loud and
didn't stop when she asked them to, she mentioned that maybe they
could go to the office. They stopped.

ANTICIPATING DISRUPTIVE BEHAVIOR

The above techniques are all ones designed to deal with
problems already present. Other techniques may be used to try
to prevent or to head off problems. (1) One such technique is
the adult organization of activities to *keep periods short*. The
children come about 9:00. About 10:00 there is a snack for
anyone who wants one. About 11:00 there is "cleanup time";
then if the weather is good everyone goes to the park. They
come back sometime after 11:30, and then it's time for

"Sesame Street" for all who want to watch it. Lunchtime is about 12:00; the children leave about 12:30. The periods of group activities, such as singing or exercising, are also kept short, with the teacher changing or terminating activities before the children get too restless:

> Started with "Twinkle, twinkle" and they knew that one fairly well. A few shouters at least make it sound like everyone's singing! Tried one or two others; had trouble with "This little light of mine" since Rose knew a different tune, we ended up singing that one without piano accompaniment; she started to teach them the words to "Freedom's comin' " but then switched to having each kid who wanted to, sing a song for the group (this was good, as attention was beginning to wander—we'd been doing this about 15 minutes and that's long enough).

(2) Besides keeping periods short, the adults *control the introduction of new activities:* they decide which days to try making playdough, operating the new "language master," or running a big cardboard-box store. On days when the children seem already excited, the store may remain "closed" but lots of puzzles are on the tables and there are many books to read. The child is guided toward a certain option before it is even presented to him.

> Rose had a cold today, was going to go home after others came to take over . . . we have store closed today (Rose's suggestion) so some chaos averted. . . . Before Rose left, she said that if it was necessary we could use just one room . . . room two since it has quieter activities going on in it.

(3) Another technique used in anticipating disruptive behavior is the use of *preemptive praise:*

> Rose asked him to help her out by watching the turtle and not letting the other children touch it since that would be hard on it. He said ok; she added, ostensibly to me but so that David could hear, 'he can be the best helper when he wants to be—he's a very good helper.'

When she was getting the kids quiet, Rose would say (of quiet
children) stuff like, "ah, he's my brother, that's the way I like to see
a brother," etc.

(4) *Promises* can also be used as a means of heading off
difficulty, but they are not used too often, primarily because
the children can exploit them too easily: either through
harassment or constant requests; or in inducing promises, then
playing one caretaker off against another. This may occur
especially in connection with the privileged position of "first in
line" walking to the park, when too many children have
received promises from different teachers that today they can
be in front. The teacher's response when a promise like this falls
through may be an apology coupled with explanation ("Oh, I'm
sorry, I didn't know that Rose had already promised Gilbert
that he could be in front"); or a further promise ("well,
tomorrow you can be in front").

In an attempt to forestall making promises which may fall
through, the teacher may handle requests by ignoring them or
by directing the child to another teacher, a version of the
leaving up in the air method mentioned above. If constant
requests have led to an implied promise, she may use direct
intervention to get the promise honored.

Wilson asked if he could be in front; meanwhile most of the kids
were running over the grass . . . continued to straggle all over, some
lying down on the sidewalk until we passed them, etc. Wilson asked
again, I said ok, you go up and ask Cheryl to let you be in front, up
with whoever was ahead at that point. He went up, came back with
his "pout" look, I asked him if he'd asked Cheryl, he said yes, but
she hadn't said anything (probably didn't even hear him or was too
busy with others); when we caught up at one corner I asked Cheryl
for him, explaining that being in front was a big deal; told Wilson to
pick a partner, he went up with Samuel, off we started again.

In this incident, the teacher was distracted by other children's
activities and would not have been able to enforce any promise:

Wilson's request was ignored in the press of other business. When he asked again, she directed him to another teacher who was at the head of the line and therefore in a position to grant his request. When this half-promise ("ok") fell through, she interceded with the other teacher to place Wilson at the head of the line.

ASSIGNING MOTIVES TO DISRUPTIVE BEHAVIOR

A guided options pattern of control is more than simply a set of tactics in the control of children. It implies, in addition, a special rhetoric of motives assumed to be the only motives that children can have. If, sociologically conceived, motives are transacted imputations of why people act as they do (Mills, 1940; Scott and Lyman, 1968), there is then the question of what "vocabulary of motives" or "accounts" seems associated with the guided options management strategy.

In the Headstart setting, practically the only motives ever assigned to disruptive behavior are those of accidents or forgetting:

At one point I heard Rose answering someone, "he just fell because it was an accident, he wasn't doing anything bad."

Having an accident or forgetting is correctable. The child can be approached with cooperative offers of assistance, reminders, requests, explanations: all sorts of guided options are available to help him out, without resorting to the necessity of labeling him an incorrigible, as one might do in more authoritarian arrangements.

also his running; we're going to have to do more than just "James, remember to walk" because it's not taking effect. Rose said we're going to have to try giving him a reminder, a warning, then the third time sit him down in a chair quiet somewhere . . . sit with him, doing a puzzle or something, until he quiets down.

The child is coached to accept this explanation of correctable motives:

> David came running into the room for lunch and was reminded to walk. One of the children said something to the effect that he always runs, he's bad; and Rose said, "no, he just forgets." David sat down, sort of tilted his head and earnestly agreed, "I just forget, is all" and Rose responded, "Yes, he just forgets, is all."

In fact, the caretaker is somewhat at a loss if the child chooses to reject this coaching and states that he did it on purpose:

> Tammy and DeeDee informed me that they knew how to dig their nails in so it hurt (so you can hardly use the old "it was an accident" routine when they're smugly explaining exactly what they did!) I semi-smoothed it over, "ooh, that can hurt someone though," mostly concentrated on soothing Aleisha.

In this instance, the caretaker's response was primarily that of leaving up in the air, with a twinge of explanation added: she quickly focused on comforting the injured child rather than on exploring the motives of the offenders. Another response might be that of offering options for the future:

> Rose replied, "from now on, James, if you want someone to get off the slide or to let you play with something, you come ask us, don't do it yourself, ok?"

Again, the motive is not emphasized, since it was neither an accident nor a lapse of memory ("I knocked him off the slide"). If it should recur, however, it could then be considered forgetting ("oh, James, you forgot to come ask us, remember?") and the motive would then be an acceptable one.

This particular rhetoric of motives appears to have three main consequences. (1) The child is being socialized into an appropriate vocabulary of motives (Mills, 1940) to be utilized in his future educational environment, a public school inculcating mostly middle-class values. ("I forgot" is a more acceptable motive than "I didn't want to do your fucking assignment.") (2) This vocabulary of excuses is used in mitigating or relieving responsibility for one's conduct. If an account is a manifestation of the underlying negotiation of identities (Scott and Lyman, 1968), then using only a vocabulary of excuses is bestowing an identity of "not-responsible" upon the child, including the assets and liabilities of that role in ongoing social interaction. (3) The child is given little opportunity self-consciously to integrate his actions with another's. Pushing because he forgot or had an accident is generally a solitary act; deliberately hitting because he wants something from someone or has been hit himself is a social act.

The possible consequences of allowing the children to claim other motives for disruptive behavior would depend on what vocabulary of motives was substituted, but would probably include the following: (1) Substitution of motives would lead to a significantly different pattern of control. If the new accounts led to negative labeling, a more authoritarian system would be likely to appear as the teachers attempted to cope with "unruly" or "bad" children. If, on the other hand, the variety of accounts were seen as allowing the child to negotiate an identity of "responsible self," more permissive interaction would take place.

(2) The new vocabulary of motives might not be as appropriate to the public school, if the "polite excuses" for one's behavior were lacking. The child might be less likely to fit into the social situation of the classroom and might be more likely to be labeled deviant in some way.

> Mrs. Adams, a kindergarten teacher in the public schools, was observing today. . . . James was building something with the domino blocks, evidently as he went by Timothy knocked them over. . . . Mrs. Adams leaned over to me and murmured, "personally, I'd put one like that in an iron cage."

(3) In a more permissive system, with its wider range of accounts, the child could have more opportunities to try out a

variety of accounts and consequent identities. Through interaction, he could learn to negotiate identities and to test their
situational appropriateness by the reactions of others (Strauss,
1959).

CONCLUSIONS

The study of a headstart classroom has suggested the
existence of a pattern of control here called the guided options
management strategy. No claim is made that this pattern
characterizes all Headstart programs or that it is characteristic
of preschool settings in general. These are questions to be
addressed in their own right.

It seems likely, indeed, that there is a variety in control
patterns, all variations falling between the extremes of authori-
tarianism and permissiveness. If we are to understand the
micro-sociological texture of schooling experiences, a prime
task is that of identifying in a close-up fashion the characteristics of these variations. It is through close, empirical accounts
that we can, perhaps, debate educational practice in more
meaningful ways than simply gross contrasts between authori-
tarianism and permissiveness.

REFERENCES

BAGLEY, W. C. (1907) Classroom Management: Its Principles and Techniques. New
    York: Macmillan.
BETTELHEIM, B. (1969) "Psychoanalysis and education." School Rev. 77: 73-86.
KOHL, H. (1969) The Open Classroom: A Practical Guide to a New Way of
    Teaching. New York: New York Review.
MILLS, C. W. (1940) "Situated actions and vocabularies of motive." Amer. Soc. Rev.
    5: 904-913.
NEILL, A. S. (1960) Summerhill: A Radical Approach to Child Rearing. New York:
    Hart.
RASBERRY, S. and R. GREENWAY (1970) Rasberry: How to Start Your Own
    School . . . and Make a Book. Freestone, Calif.: Freestone.
SCOTT, M. B. and S. M. LYMAN (1968) "Accounts." Amer. Soc. Rev. 33: 46-62.
STRAUSS, A. L. (1959) Mirrors and Masks. New York: Free Press.

LACHLAN McCLENAHEN is currently a staff analyst with the California State Department of Health.

JOHN LOFLAND is Professor of Sociology at the University of California, Davis. He is the founding editor of *Urban Life.* Professor Lofland's most recent books are *State Executions* (with Horace Bleackly) and *Doing Social Life: The Qualitative Study of Human Interaction in Natural Settings.*

Bearing Bad News

TACTICS OF THE
DEPUTY U.S. MARSHAL

LACHLAN McCLENAHEN
Department of Health
State of California

JOHN LOFLAND
Department of Sociology
University of California, Davis

Life is punctuated by bad news. People die, become crippled, maimed, and chronically ill; they lose their fortunes, souls, self-esteem, spouses, offspring, and friends to death or other humans. Bad news and potentials for its occurrence are woven tightly into the fabric of social life, certain to be visited upon virtually everyone on many occasions.

Authors' Note: *The editorial and substantive suggestions of Lyn H. Lofland are gratefully acknowledged.*

It is of signal interest that modern humans are not always direct witnesses to events that bring them grief. It not infrequently happens in complex societies that when unhappy events transpire, those most affected by their occurrence do not witness them, or if they do are unable correctly to interpret them and/or to assess their implications. In those cases, it becomes necessary for a second party to communicate the bad news to its target. Such people are, in the everyday language, "bearers of bad news." All of us are likely to have been bearers of bad news on one or more occasions. It therefore belabors the obvious to point out that the role is usually unpleasant—sometimes highly unpleasant. The nature and sources of the unpleasantness are not, however, the same for all bearers, two broad kinds of which need to be distinguished: those who enact the role in their private lives (amateurs), and those who perform it as a part of their work or occupation. The two differ importantly in ways in which they are likely to relate to the recipient of the bad news. Amateur bearers seem more likely to be concerned with the trauma their news may cause the recipient; occupational bearers tend to be more concerned with avoiding "scenes" initiated by emotionally disturbed recipients. Amateur bearers worry about the impact bad news will have upon its target; occupational bearers worry about the impact the news will have upon themselves. Such tendencies are, of course, just that: tendencies rather than mutually exclusive features.

This report focuses upon one instance of occupational bearers of bad news, the deputy U.S. Marshal, a role involving, among other tasks, delivering Summons/Complaints, taking federally accused into custody, and delivering the convicted to prison.[1] Occupants of this role, that is, frequently deliver bad news. The deputy Marshal is, therefore, a strategic site for the study of how occupational (and other) bearers manage bad news encounters. More specifically, the deputy Marshal is an instance of the class of situation where bad news is occupationally delivered *between strangers*. Moreover, while here we focus on the deputy

Marshal, we will also be pointing out similarities with other bearers of bad news reported in the accumulating literature on this generic situation.

I. THE SITUATION OF BAD NEWS

Deputy Marshals tend to bring three main concerns to the situation of bearing bad news; they define their situation along three dimensions of the problematic. While these are specific to deputies, their more general relevance will be evident.

First, they are concerned that recipients do not hold them personally responsible for the bad news they bring. As in the tales of rulers who beheaded messengers bringing news of military defeat, deputies believed recipients too often failed to separate the news from the vehicle of its conveyance. This was a concern to avoid the moral taint of delivering bad news and seemed to derive, in part, from the associated and larger cultural belief that it is rather immoral to bring another person to grief (cf. Tesser, Rosen, and Batchelor, 1972). Rather similar to historic state executioners who asked condemned to forgive them (Bleackly and Lofland, 1976), deputies desired to get themselves "off the hook" with recipients. Second, recipients became emotionally distraught with a frequency sufficient to concern deputies that the former would not "keep their cool." Crying, stumbling, and resisting recipients complicated their day's work and, moreover, gave rise to the possibility of complaint to superiors that deputies did not deal tactfully and discretely with the situation. This is a micro version of the larger problem of "cooling the mark out" (Goffman, 1952). Third, overtly distraught recipients could create problems for deputies in controlling their own emotions. As agents of a federal bureaucracy, they were obligated to be emotionally neutral and composed, but as witnesses to "heavy scenes" they feared they might find themselves feeling stronger emotions, be these sympathetic or antipathetic (cf. the class of situations addressed by Coombs and Goldman, 1973). They were concerned to forestall the development of situations where such emotions might become a difficulty.

II. PHASES AND TACTICS OF BEARING BAD NEWS

Leaving aside various techniques of avoiding the situation altogether (e.g., passing the buck, physical avoidance, and so on), what are ways in which communication of bad news is managed? Management practices are usefully divided into their three, main, sequential phases: techniques of preparing (getting ready), delivering (actually doing it), and shoring (dealing with the recipient after he or she knows the bad news). Of course, many techniques are multiphasic; they can be and are used in all three moments of the bad news event. We here emphasize prime or first usage, recognizing that a given technique might also be used in later stages.

A. PREPARING

1. *Distancing.* Although not intended in the sense of deputies having much direct and strategic control over them, several aspects of their situation operated at the structural and preparatory level to alleviate the stress of bearing bad news. These preparatory alleviations all served to increase the social *distance* between bearer and recipient, a distance existing prior to their actual, face-to-face encounter. As such, these are *functional* rather than fully intentional tactics. First, the people to whom they delivered bad news were overwhelmingly *strangers* to them—people with whom they had no complicating, emotional involvements. On the rare and fortuitous occasions when deputies did encounter someone they knew, troubles tended to ensue:

I was walking through the holding cell area of the office and somebody yelled: "Hey, Larry!" I look around and—Jesus Christ—it's my old buddy Phil! I said: "Hey, Man . . . what the fuck are you doin' back there behind those bars?" He said: "They busted me, Man." I said: "For what?" "Draft-dodgin," he said. "Oh, goddam." This was really bad, you know, because Phil was a real good friend. We had run around together a lot in school. Well, I spent the rest of the day back there keeping the guy company and supplying him with coffee and cigarettes. Had to give some to the rest of the prisoners too. Man, they never had it so good! Then, later that day, I had to take him before the magistrate to be arraigned. Our Marshal was one of these rule-crazy bastards and made me handcuff him. That really got me . . . I was really embarrassed. Phil told me not to worry about it; that it was just my job. But it really got me . . . I'll never forget it.

In another case, the deputy had to deliver two convicted friends to county jail:

When we were riding down there [a distance of about 60 miles] we were having a hell of a time—laughing and telling jokes. But the closer we got to the jail, the quieter it got. Jesus, by the time we got there, Bob [the other deputy] and I were really feeling shitty. We really felt bad about putting those guys in that jail. They knew we were feeling bad and told us not to worry about it, that it had to be done, and they were the ones who had screwed up. But we still felt like shit.

Such tactical preference for strangers is found among other occupational bearers, as with family doctors who avoid telling patients their child has polio, shunting the task off to stranger-M.D.'s at clinics and hospitals where the child becomes a patient (Davis, 1963: 30, 1972: 92-103). Second, it is tactical in the sense of increasing social distance and thereby decreasing emotional involvement that deputies tended to be white, working and lower-middle-class, and somewhat educated while recipients of the bad news they bore tended to be lower than they in the race/class/education rankings of American society. Indeed, the work of some deputies became more emotionally difficult in the sixties as draft evasion and resistance cases loomed larger in their work load, bringing recipients closer to their own world (and sometimes higher than their location, which again increased distance). Bad news bearers in medical settings sometimes exploit this same kind of tactical distance. Glaser and Strauss (1968, 1965) and Sudnow (1967) imply that middle-class patients in private hospitals tend not be told they are dying; lower class patients in public hospitals tend to be told (in, moreover, relatively abrasive fashion).

Two physical aspects of preparation function to increase distance or, in their absence, to reduce it and complicate bearers' tasks. First, viewed generically the physical setting itself varies in its tactical protectiveness along the dimensions of the degree to which it is formal, august, impersonal, and foreboding (as are court rooms and jails) versus informal, homey, private, and inviting (as private dwellings can tend to be). As a general proposition, because of the greater distance provided, bad news tends to be staged in, and occupational bearers, at least, have a preference for, more foreboding and formal settings of delivery. Deputy Marshals operated in both kinds of settings and tended to suffer or get-by correspondingly. Second, the coverings and labelings of the human body itself vary along these same dimensions. Robes, uniforms (including badges, guns, and complex utility belts), and distinctive titles ("Your Honor," "Officer," "Deputy") are tactical conveyances of distance. Indeed, their police users often quite consciously believe that their paramilitary adornments have a value quite beyond their immediate and narrow utility—they "command respect." The deputy Marshal was a plainclothes policeman, a distancing disadvantage, one that was not overcome by their studiedly casual openings of suit coats to reveal holstered pistols.

2. *Presaging.* One important class of preparatory tactics was not available to deputies because of their role as formal agents of government, but needs to be treated nonetheless

owing to its prevalence in less restrictive circumstances of bearing bad news. Among medical bearers, especially, the stage of preparing for the actual bad news encounter consists importantly of *presaging,* of dribbling out facts and pieces of information over time that "lead up to" and "make the way for" the actual bad news. The previously dribbled out facts can then be assigned evidentiary meaning in the bad news encounter itself. Indeed, the hope may be that the recipient will discover the bad news for himself, that the emergent facts will "speak for themselves." In such a manner, medical bearers may hope that by the time they actually have to talk to the recipient about the bad news of his health, he will already have perceived, digested, and resigned himself to the facts of his case. The bad news encounter becomes then only an "official" confirmation of what has already been "seen." The rationale of this tactic is, of course, avoidance of traumatizing the recipient by disclosing shocking news for which he has not had a chance to prepare himself.[2] In the substantively different but generically identical setting of the modern junior college, the eventual bad news for large numbers of students that they are not going to achieve B.A. degrees and are to become "terminal" A.A.'s is carefully presaged by means of a complex and prolonged examination, counseling, and documenting process, Burton Clark (1960) reports.

B. DELIVERING

Occupational bearers of bad news differ from amateurs in, by definition, the frequency with which they perform the act of delivery. Deputy Marshals visit bad news on people several times in their typical day, day after day. That situational fact underlay and prompted their central interaction tactic for imparting their unhappy information: the tactic of *"it's just routine."* It is important to distinguish two forms of "it's just routine," only one of which is at present germane. Social psychologically, deputies managed their relation to their own *private feelings* in good part by such a definition[3] but putting that aside, the bad news was treated in a mundane manner *in the delivering interaction*. That is, at least initially, deputies acted as if the recipient had or ought to have an attitude similar to his own, e.g., "this is just another instance of this or that charge or court action." The matter at hand was a commonplace—it happened to all kinds of people all the time—and was therefore no cause for alarm, confusion, or embarrassment. The news was thus "normalized," as with subpoenae: "Oh, we serve thousands of these things, it's really nothing to worry about."

The effort, though, is to make the *event* seem normal and routine rather than to imply the event was normal for the recipient who, in the case of subpoenae, was likely to affect naiveté and hence purity in legal matters. The following exchange involving service in a criminal case illustrates normalizing while protecting the recipient's pose of purity:

Deputy: Hi. Jim Martin?

Recip.: Uh . . . yeah. Why?

Deputy: I'm Bob Thomas, Deputy U.S. Marshal. I have a subpoena here for you. [hands the paper to him]

Recip.: Subpoena?! I haven't done anything . . . I don't know anything. What's this all about?

Deputy: Let's see. [looks at subpoena] This is the case of the U.S.A. vs. Robertson. As I recall, that's a theft of government property case. I guess the U.S. Attorney thinks your testimony can be of some help in clearing up the case.

Recip.: Hell, I don't know anything. I don't know how to testify . . . I don't even know how to get to court. Do I have to do this?

Deputy: Yes, you do. But don't worry. If you don't know anything, then they aren't likely to put you on the stand. If you do go on, all you have to do is answer a few questions . . . no big deal. Before I leave, I'll draw you a map to get you to the courthouse.

Recip.: Jeez . . . I don't know.

Deputy: Relax. You're the fourteenth person I've subpoenaed in this case. I'm sure you know a lot of the guys there. Don't worry, cases like this come up all the time. Oh, by the way. You will be paid $20 per day for each day you are required to be in court. You will also get $16 extra if you're required to stay overnight, and 10 cents per mile to and from court to your home.

As the above dialogue shows, the brute moment of delivery was quite brief—lasting only a few seconds—before being supplanted by problems of dealing with the possibility of untoward or "sticky" behavior on the part of the recipient.

C. SHORING

In order to forestall uncontrolled behavior and to contain it if it occurred, deputies engaged in "shoring" operations, tactics directed to "supporting [recipients] with or as if with a prop," to use the phraseology of a dictionary. Shoring tactics moved along two main lines: manipulation of the configuration of items making up the bad news and contrivance of supportive (or at least mitigating) emotional stances and attitudes in the interaction.

1. *Manipulating the News.* Any bad news is itself a complicated amalgam of units of information, implications, and fears. The central, defining or core piece of bad news is itself variable in its meaning—the nature and degree of its "badness"—as a function of the context in which it is set. This fact provided deputies a degree of manipulative leverage over the context and meaning of the bad news. There were two main types of shoring tactics: scaling down the badness and playing up the goodness.

a. Tactics of scaling down the badness pointed out contextual aspects of the news that made it seem less onerous than the fears of the recipient might otherwise rampantly fantasize.

(i) The most common and forthright version of this was the "educational" process of showing how *"it's not as bad as you think."* In the following dialogue between two deputies and a prisoner in an automobile, we see the deputies intimating jail is not a picnic, but then it is not too bad either. Jail may not be inevitable; there are the alternatives of release on bail or one's own recognizance. In the event of conviction (which is presented as uncertain), the final disposition of the case is relatively bright—especially when contrasted with the dispositions of a neighboring jurisdiction. Through such "shoring" of their captive, they seek to relieve his anxiety and depression—and hence their own situation.

Prisoner: Hey, you guys goin' to put me in jail when we get to [the city]?

1st Dep.: Yeah. At least for a little while. Think you can make the bail . . . it's a thousand bucks.

Prisoner: [becoming agitated] Jeez . . . a thousand dollars. I don't know anyone with a thousand dollars. [pause] What's the jail like?

2nd Dep.: Never been in jail before, huh? [prisoner nods] Well, it's not too bad. Not a whole lot of fun, of course, but not too bad. Besides, you may not have to go to jail even if you can't make bail.

Prisoner: Oh, yeah? [pause. Other conversation]

Prisoner: Hey, what did you mean when you said I might not have to go to jail even though I couldn't make bail?

2nd Dep.: Well, if you have a good record and it looks like you will probably show up for your court appearances . . . the Magistrate might release you on your O.R.

Prisoner: What's O.R.?

2nd Dep.: It means you're out on your "own recognizance." You sign a form promising to show up for court when you're supposed to. Now if you sign and you don't show . . . it's a new rap and can cost you 5 and 5.

Prisoner: 5 and 5 what?

2nd Dep.: 5 years or $5,000 or both. If you do get O.R'd, I'd advise you to make those court appearances.

Prisoner: You think I can make this O.R.?

2nd Dep.: Well . . . I don't know. You say you've never been in jail before . . . ever been arrested?

Prisoner: No.

2nd Dep.: You lived in this area [small town] very long?

Prisoner: About two years.

2nd Dep.: Un-huh . . . at the same address?

Prisoner: No. I've lived at a couple of places. . . . you know.

2nd Dep.: Un-huh . . . your family live around here?

Prisoner: Yeah my mother lives here. And my two sisters. They've lived here for quite a while.

2nd Dep.: Un-huh . . . well, you might make it. Sure doesn't hurt to try. We've got you on a pretty petty beef . . . your record doesn't sound bad . . . yeah, I wouldn't be surprised if you did.

Prisoner: [somewhat later] How much time do you think I'll get?

2nd Dep.: Hey, Man . . . you're not even *convicted* yet. Maybe you'll beat the rap.

Prisoner: Yeah. [pauses] But if I don't . . . how much time will I get?

2nd Dep.: Well, that's hard to say. That depends on your record, the judge, the probation officer's report, your attorney . . . a lot of things. But I'd say not too much. They're pretty soft on draft-dodgers in [the city]. Now if this were [another city] you'd get two years straight time in the joint. It's not that tough here. In fact, if you've got a good record and you impress the judge and the probation officer who handles your case, you might get off with straight probation, which puts you right back on the bricks again. Now I'm not saying you'll get probation . . . it all depends on you and the judge.

2nd Dep.: [after a long silence] Do you have an attorney?

Prisoner: No.

2nd Dep.: Can you afford to hire one?

Prisoner: I don't have any money.

2nd Dep.: No problem. Tell that to the Magistrate when you're arraigned this afternoon and he'll appoint one for you—won't cost you anything.

Prisoner: Hey, that's alright!

(ii) When the news is irrefutably and unequivocally bad—as bad as you think!—there remains the possibility that *"it could have been worse."* Thus, in transporting the convicted to federal prisons, deputies typically made note of ways in which federal were superior to state prisons.

[Scene: automobile containing two deputies and three prisoners. Prisoners are shackled at wrists and ankles and chained together. Prisoners ride in back, deputies in front.]

1st. Dep.: [to prisoners as a group] You ever been in a federal joint before? [two prisoners say that they have, one indicates he has not] Well, you [addressing one of the veteran prisoners] have to admit that the federal joints are the best places to do time.

Vet. Pris: Yeah, they're not so bad. They really feed good. And the industries are pretty good too.

1st Dep.: Lots better than the state, right?

Vet. Pris: Oh, hell yeah! Those state joints ain't for shit. Too many guys tryin' to shove a shank into ya—for nothin'. Food isn't near as good either. Besides, in this state, they have that goddam "indeterminate sentence" so a guy doesn't know when he'll get out. Some bastard gets it in for you, and you might never get out. It can be a pure sonofabitch!

2nd. Dep.: Yeah. You guys go along with the program at the joint you're goin' to, and you won't have any problems. You guys all have A-2 numbers . . . so you can get paroled at any time. Keep straight and you've got it made. Right Jones? [to the other veteran prisoner]

Vet. Pris: Yeah, it's not so bad if you don't fuck-up. If some screw doesn't get on your ass. I'm goin' to get my shit together and keep it together this trip, get out early, and get a job. I've had it.

2nd Dep.: Yeah, the best thing to do is to go along with the program.

It is of note that the veteran prisoners in this dialogue join with the deputy in defining their situation as better than it might have been. Such "collusions" were not rare and suggest, indeed, a strong need to so believe.

(iii) Even if news is not as bad as one thinks and could have been worse, it can still be onerous if it is going to go on for a long time and without hope of ending. Bad news, that is, is less bad if it is *temporary* and/or *reversible*. During transport of the convicted to prison, deputies were prone to treat short sentences as insignificant or ridiculous with such statements as: "You can do this dab of time standing on your head"; "It's hardly worth the drive to jail, but to keep the records straight." Long sentences were usually treated as reversible. Prisoners were almost invariably asked if they intended to appeal their conviction and if the reply was in the negative, they were likely to be encouraged to change their minds.

> [Scene: deputy conversing with two prisoners just sentenced to 20 years for armed bank robbery. They are being escorted from court to a holding cell.]
>
> Deputy: You guys goin' to appeal your case? Think the judge made any mistakes in the trial?
>
> Prisoner: Oh, I don't know. Maybe. Yeah, I might.
>
> Deputy: Yeah, you can't lose anything by tryin'. I know I would if I were you. You guys know Punch over at the jail?
>
> Prisoner: Punch? Yeah, I know him . . . he's the guy out of Leavenworth who's appealing the bank beef here. Says he's going to beat it.
>
> Deputy: Well, I think he has a pretty good chance of doing it. In fact, he probably will. So you never know 'til you try in this kind of a deal.[4]

The tactic of temporariness is of course widely used. Doctors hold out the hope of discovery of new techniques and medicines with which to correct present disorders. Attorneys hold out possibilities of winning appeals. Mothers tell their children that their bumps and bruises will only hurt for a little while. The bearer tells the recipient, in effect: "Cheer up, things are going to get better." Indeed, with the possible exception of death, a skilled bearer can construe any condition as merely temporary.

(iv) Finally, deputies manipulated the context of the core bad news through *auspicious omission* of the worst implications of the consequences. With convicted prisoners in transport to prison, questions of sex-life in those institutions were carefully avoided by deputies. When it was necessary to house prisoners overnight in especially uncomfortable and "raunchy" jails, that news was not provided beforehand. The more unpleasant contextual facts that deputies wanted to avoid, however, were not denied if pressed for by a prisoner. Rather, the necessity sometimes to interact with prisoners over several hours or even days prompted them to safe claims of ignorance of unpleasant aspects they actually knew or to quick passing over of such aspects in a light-hearted, bantering manner.

b. Tactics of playing-up the positive sought to point out how the bad news might well have been a "blessing in disguise." Even prison may have constructive things to offer, a possibility that some prisoners as much as deputies elaborated in the hours after their convictions.

[Scene: car enroute to federal prison with a newly sentenced "novice" prisoner who faces a 2-year term]

Prisoner: Say, I hear these federal joints are pretty good . . . you know, the food and all.

1st Dep.: Yeah, they feed better than any other joint.

Prisoner: I hear the industry is pretty good too. Maybe I can learn a trade while I'm in.

2nd Dep.: That's a good idea. Damn hard to make a living on the outside without a trade . . . besides, you can build up a pile of money to tide you over until you can find a job after you're out.

Prisoner: Yeah, if a guy doesn't waste his time, he can do O.K. in a joint. Another thing I can do is lift weights. I've always wanted to build myself up. I hear they have lots of equipment.

2nd Dep.: They do. That seems to be pretty popular with the guys.

Among other bearers, such as medical ones, playing up the positive may be framed to the relatives of a just-dead patient in terms of how extensive tissue damage, deterioration, hopeless prognosis, excessive pain, or the like, make it "better" that the patient died. That which is usually bad news—death—thus becomes better than what is usually good news—life. Clergymen and funeral directors appear to specialize in a more general version of this tactic: people "pass on" to a "better life," "know blessed relief from trials and sorrows," and so forth.[5]

2. *Mitigating Emotions in Interaction.* Manipulation of the news is accompanied by an *attitude* toward the situation and the recipient. In the delivery phase, the prime attitude was an impersonal "it's just routine." As the situation itself became more varied in the shoring phase, so did the range of attitudinal stances affected by deputies as devices through which to control recipients.

a. One of these attitudinal stances pointedly separated deputies as *persons* from the *actions* they undertook. Deputies were brought into close and recipient-demeaning physical and social contact with their charges. Prisoners had often to be fingerprinted, photographed, handcuffed, shackled, led into and/or out of jails, prisons, automobiles, airports, restaurants, and restrooms. Their persons had to be searched. They could eat, smoke, drink, or telephone only at narrowly specified times and places. The array of these confinements made up a microtexture of on-going bad news that deputies had to manage in the context of the larger bad news that prisoners already knew. Deputies strove to mitigate the demeanments of these confinements and help both their charges and themselves save face through *unsolicited* explanations that *regulations required* such measures. Impersonal "D.C." (District of Columbia) bureaucracy was to blame; the deputy was powerless to act otherwise and he had a moral obligation to perform the duties of his office. In such a manner, the concrete human bodies involved were set apart from the impersonal roles each was enacting. Therefore, neither of them ought to become personally distraught over the transpiring, demeaning events. Thus, also, in response to requests:

I'm sorry—you can't smoke in the car, it's against regulations.

I can't get you a Coke—it's not allowed.

Yeah, I know that's a lot of iron [waist to wrist to ankle shackles], but D.C. makes us do it—be my ass if I didn't.

Importantly, deputies resisted citing charges or convictions as justification for these confinements. A prisoner was chained-up, for example, not because he robbed a bank and engaged in a gun-battle with his captors, but because regulations specified that all prisoners being transported by automobile had to be restrained in such a manner. Only (the rare) prisoner who most persistently challenged the legitimacy of the restrictions got told something like: "Well, if you don't like it [the regulations], maybe you shouldn't have robbed the bank . . . that's going to mean a lot of things you won't like."

The effort of deputies, then, was to avoid if, at all possible, appearing themselves morally to blame the people on whom they visited bad news. In this way, they eased threats to dignity.

b. Prisoners themselves differed in the degree of experience they had with this deputy-dominated situation and its brand of bad news. Deputies believed less experienced prisoners (e.g., first-time offenders) were more threatened by being taken into custody and that they were more likely to break down in crying, to blow-up in rage, or otherwise to resist "processing" through fingerprinting and the rest. In order to inhibit these possibilities, inexperienced prisoners, especially, were treated to *hyperconspicuous* displays of deputies seeming to be engaged in a *boring routine.* By making the situation seem so normal that it was an utter bore, deputies hoped given prisoners would also be stimulated to be merely normal.

A set of routinized and (to deputies) stale *quips and jokes* used at more acute moments of demeanment were an important element of this hypernormality. It is likely that all bearers of bad news have their own versions of what is known classically as "gallows humor" and among deputies such tension-releasing gambits assumed forms like these:

When shackling prisoners:

Deputy: O.K., gang. It's time to put on all the beautiful hardware the U.S. government has imported to California for your pleasure and amusement. Ah, yes . . . now who will be first?

When "mugging":

Deputy: O.K. Now I want to take a few shots at you . . . with the camera, that is. Let's start with the front. O.K. that's lookin' good! Now, let's get your profile. Say, if these turn out good, would you like to order some? I can give you a dozen 8 X 10 glossies for a mere $25.

When finger-printing:

Deputy: Right. Now, just relax your hand. Let me do all the work. First time you've been printed, huh? I can tell because you're trying to help me roll the fingers. Just relax. And . . . a very nice set of prints, if I do say so. [to another deputy in the area] Hey, Joe . . . why is it we only get good prints from guys we'll never see again?[6]

c. On occasion, a recipient would begin to break down and cry or to blow up in rage. At the incipient stage, deputies, with restraint, encouraged such a prisoner to "pull himself together." If the discomposure of upset or agitation remained relatively mild and controlled, deputies were prone to act "as if nothing had happened," to disregard the discomposure and thereby provide the recipient an opportunity to recover lost face without the penalty of open disrespect from deputies. Deputies subtly offered, that is, to

disregard the just past collapse or outburst if the recipient
would then "pull himself together." Such offers usually
worked quickly or not at all. When they did not, the prisoner
was punished or placated at the price of lost "face" and
respect:

> Prisoner: [clearly agitated] You guys aren't going to put me in
> that place [meaning the county jail] are you?
>
> Deputy: Yeah. We're going to take you over in a few minutes.
>
> Prisoner: [tears beginning to form] But I've got a bad heart. It'll
> kill me. I won't get a bunk tonight . . . the jail's too crowded. I'll
> have to sleep on the floor. [begins to sob openly]
>
> Deputy: Hey! Take it easy. Hey, pull yourself together. Jesus
> Christ! [disgustedly] Hey! Come on, now.
>
> Prisoner: [sobbing brokenly now] I just can't take it any-
> more . . . I just can't take it anymore . . . I'm all worn out . . . I
> just can't.
>
> Deputy: Hey! Jesus Christ, Man—pull yourself together. Come
> on now, be a man.
>
> Prisoner: [still crying] I don't care [presumably about judgments
> of his conduct] . I can't help it . . . I just can't take it anymore.
>
> Deputy: [to colleague with heavy sarcasm, disgust, and a dash of
> wry humor] He can't take it anymore . . . hell, I can't take it
> anymore! [to prisoner] O.K., relax. O.K., O.K. [again to
> colleague] Let's try to make this crybaby happy. Call the jail and
> see if they can get this dude a bunk. It's too late to go the South
> County tonight, but if they can't fix him up here, I'll take him
> down tomorrow morning [a Saturday] . [to prisoner] O.K., O.K.
> goddammit. We're going to fix you up. We'll get you to South
> County tomorrow [which is where the prisoner said he wanted to
> go] . I know this is rough, but you've got to be a man.

III. CONCLUSIONS

This report is intended as a specific and delimited
contribution to the larger and longer-term study of the
generic or formal situation of delivering bad news. As such,
detailed and systematic comparison with other inquiries

addressed to this same situation must be performed in order properly to generate grounded generalizations and conclusions. Since a body of inquiries adequate to this task on the present situation does not yet exist, any conclusions offered must be mere conjecture, tenaciously to be distrusted.[7]

1. We have reported prominent moments and tactics of bearing bad news among deputy U.S. Marshals. Overall, these tactics make up a strategy we might call "nice guy impersonality." Deputies were not "involved" and "judgmental," on the one side, nor strictly impersonal and "uninvolved," on the other. Their orientation to accomplishing a minimally complicated and "sticky" day, combined with their fears about recipient behavior, gave rise to mild forms of emotional involvement, mostly of the "nice guy" variety. Nice guy impersonality is only one type of interactional strategy in bearing bad news. The on-going study of the generic situation of bad news requires delineation of other fundamental strategies (with their microtactical components) and specification of the larger social organizational contexts in which they appear. Thus, nice-guy impersonality appears most congruent with contexts in which bearers and recipients do not have enduring and intimate relations. Longer-term and more personal relations between bearers and recipients of bad news seem more likely to generate much higher levels of emotional arousal and distress of either a highly sympathetic or condemning kind (as in, for example, a parole officer having to inform a well-known and liked parolee he must return to prison).

2. Occupational bearers of bad news tend either to benefit from impersonal "distancing" arrangements such as sheer stranger relations and the impersonality of some physical settings and uniforms, or to construct distance with devices available to manipulation as in defining the event as something less than its worst news. The latter is apparent in the "it's just routine" definition used by deputy Marshals and in the practice among coroners of saying "That's not a body lying there. It's an *investigation*" (Charmaz, 1975: 304).

Contexts that permit and sustain such definitions require specification. Moreover, what are consequences of circumstances in which it is not possible to deescalate the worst? The propensity of everyone to pass the delivery of bad news to someone else if at all possible suggests, for example, that sheer avoidance is a a likely maneuver.

3. Under conditions of even the very least leeway occupational bearers of bad news are prone to "build up to"—to presage—the news. Charmaz reports that even in the impersonality of coroner telephone announcements of death, the relative is given "a few clues of lesser weight before getting to the point of the call." Some try even to "lead the relative into questioning *them* . . . [setting] the conditions wherein [they] . . . can impart progressively unpromising news" (Charmaz, 1975: 312-313). Presaging is not, nonetheless, universal either in opportunities for its use or of the propensity to use it. What are its limits and contexts?

4. In the interactional strategy of nice-guy impersonality several devices are used to manipulate the news itself by scaling down the badness (e.g., "it's not as bad as you think," "it could have been worse," "it's temporary") or playing up the positive. These are only a few microtactical possibilities from a much larger set and they are likely confined to only certain strategies such as that of nice-guy impersonality. Other inquires and comparisons should show other possibilities and the limits of their occurrence.

5. The components of emotional neutrality and impartiality so salient to bureaucratic roles seem to furnish occupants strategically usable emotions for the delivering of bad news. "It's just routine" is an auspiciously available emotional display for the moment of delivery. In shoring, exhibitions of self-protective rule-compliance, boring routine, and studied inattention to distress are interactional resources doubtless drawn from learnings about how agents of bureaucracies—especially the American federal bureaucracy—ought properly to act. Not all bearers of bad news have such role-imagery resources available for use in displaying miti-

gating emotions. Upon what other kinds of imageries are such bearers forced to draw?

6. How bad the news actually is within the shared value-systems of bearers and recipients is a variable that importantly contextualizes the pattern we have reported. Set in a continuum of degree of badness, deputy Marshals seem to deal largely in "mid-range" bad news. They made neither announcements of death or catastrophic illness, on the more severe side, nor announcements of the milder vexations of ordinary life, on the less severe side. That fact likely contributes to the relative ease of their nice-guy impersonality and structures situations of bad news announcements in general.

Again, it is our conviction that the best social scientific accounts of, and generalizations about, generic social situations are constructed from intensive comparisons of multiple inquiries of an intensive kind. Since we do not yet have sufficient such studies on the situation of bad news, generalizations must be made with extreme caution and are likely premature.

NOTES

1. The senior author was employed part-time as a deputy U.S. Marshal over the years 1967-1973. Deputies worked in shifting pairs and during that period he was associated with some thirty deputies in delivering bad news as well as interacting and being with many others in a wide variety of settings. For a nine month period in 1971-1972, deputy activities were made a concerted object of sociological scrutiny and field note accumulation. The larger perspective informing this report is elaborated in Lofland (forthcoming).

2. Glaser and Strauss (1965, 1968). When the bad news is unavoidably sudden, some doctors nonetheless strive in bad news encounters to set the episode in a cumulation, build-up format on the theory that such a form is more understandable, Sudnow (1967: 118-125) relates.

3. This self-management tactic is rather common in stressful occupations. See, for example, Coombs and Goldman, 1973; Charmaz, 1975: 303.

4. In cases of long sentences, deputies were especially concerned that prisoners might become desperate enough to "try something" (i.e., escape or suicide) that would greatly complicate their tasks, hence this specific kind of encouragement.

5. Playing up the positive cuts, however, two ways in many circumstances, especially those of death. A doctor who tells a surviving son "Hey, great news . . . your father's dead . . . think of all the money you are going to inherit" is obviously being *too* positive.

6. Chains and handcuffs were often banteringly referred to as "jewelry," and jails as "hotels" and "homes." Such *muffled language* serves the additional function of obscuring the reality of the bad news and thereby easing the situation. It is akin to the medical doctor who answers the question "Is it cancer?" with "We don't call it that," proceeding to a technical terminology the patient understands only vaguely (Glaser and Strauss, 1965: 124). On "language alteration" and euphemisms more generally in situations of bad news, see Coombs and Goldman (1973) and Glaser and Strauss (1968).

7. The inductive and consolidating view of theory construction espoused here is elaborated in Glaser and Strauss (1967: ch. 5, "From Substantive to Formal Theory") and Lofland (forthcoming: ch. 7, "Consolidating").

REFERENCES

BLEACKLY, H. and J. LOFLAND (1976) State Executions Viewed Historically and Sociologically. Montclair, N.J.: Patterson Smith.

CHARMAZ, K. C. (1975) "The coroner's strategies for announcing death." Urban Life 4 (October): 296-316.

CLARK, B. (1960) "The cooling-out function in higher education." Amer. J. of Sociology 65 (May): 569-576.

COOMBS, R. H. and L. GOLDMAN (1973) "Maintenance and discontinuity of coping mechanisms in an intensive care unit." Social Problems 20 (Winter): 342-355.

DAVIS, F. (1972) Illness, Interaction, and the Self. Belmont, Calif.: Wadsworth.

––– (1963) Passage Through Crisis. Indianapolis: Bobbs-Merrill.

GLASER, B. G. and A. L. STRAUSS (1968) Time for Dying. Chicago: Aldine.

––– (1967) The Discovery of Grounded Theory. Chicago: Aldine.

––– (1965) Awareness of Dying. Chicago: Aldine.

GOFFMAN, E. (1952) "On cooling the mark out." Psychiatry 15 (November): 451-463.

LOFLAND, J. (forthcoming) The Qualitative Study of Social Interaction in Natural Settings. New York: John Wiley.

SUDNOW, D. (1967) Passing On. Englewood Cliffs, N.J.: Prentice-Hall.

TESSER, A., S. ROSEN, and T. R. BATCHELOR (1972) "On the reluctance to communicate bad news (the MUM effect): a role play extension." J. of Personality 40 (March): 88-103.

41610